THE CASH-FLOW BREAKFAST CLUB

A Story and A Manual

THE CASH-FLOW BREAKFAST CLUB

A Story and A Manual

by Omni Casey & Chara Casey

The story of you... And how a leap of faith to attend a unique investor meet-up changes everything. From zero passive income to complete financial freedom in five years or less.

The Story used to illustrate the investment strategies described in this book is fictional. Names, characters, places, and incidents either are the product of the author's imagination or are used fictitiously. Any resemblance to actual persons, living or dead, events, or locales is entirely coincidental.

First paperback edition, May 2022
ISBN 979-8-9857348-0-5

Table of Contents

Acknowledgments

Showing is better than telling. The first time I attempted to write this book several years ago, it was an autobiography that read like an instruction manual. It was very short and was straight to the point. As a high D personality, I am often accused of thinking and talking in bullet points, so it naturally made sense that my book would be that way also. It turns out that although the principles were valuable, and the lessons shared were beneficial, it was not a book that I would have been proud of. So, after shelving my first draft for a few years, I was recently inspired to completely rewrite this book, and I partnered with my wife to provide the lessons in a power parable format that we ultimately hope would be more relatable and entertaining for you, the reader. You are about to immerse yourself in a story loaded with actionable content. Though all characters, scenes, and scenarios are fictional, and any references to real people and actual events are unintended, all lessons, results, and testimonials are based on the true accounts pulled from the life of the authors, real estate investors, real estate agents and coaching clients that they have helped. Thank you for letting us be a part of your life. Just like the main characters in this book who go through several life-changing discoveries throughout their journey to financial freedom, you will find there are simple steps and true principles that you can implement in your life to become financially free through real estate investing. We strongly believe that no matter where you are financially right now, you can follow these steps and principles to design a life of financial freedom through cash-flow real estate investing. Thank you for inviting us in on your journey.

CHAPTER 1:

Living Under a Bridge

THE EVICTION

Is this what homeless is? Dan thought as he watched the property manager lock the door behind them as they exited his apartment and home for the last two and a half years. He could just imagine the headline now: "One of Honolulu's top real estate agents, now homeless!" It seemed just like yesterday that Dan and Karen had moved in. The excitement, the prestige that came with that address. Living in the "penthouse" of one of Honolulu's premier luxury apartments came with its perks. Every morning, the sunrise views were Instagram-worthy, #BlessedLife. It made Dan cringe as he thought back to his nearly daily morning post from his lanai. *And now? I'm on the waiting list for a spot at one of the cheapest apartments around.* There are no "tracks" in Hawaii, but if there were, he would be moving to the other side of them. To add insult to injury, he didn't even know when he would be able to move in.

Of course, at that very moment, Dan wasn't homeless yet, as he had friends and family who would more than welcome him until he secured a new place, but the thought of asking anyone for help, the thought of even telling anyone that things were this bad, just seemed out of the question for Dan. So many things were racing through his head. It had been six months since Karen, his longtime girlfriend, announced to the world on social media that she had left him. *If everyone found out that I lost "the penthouse," they would all think it was a direct result of Karen leaving. Oh, she would just love that, thought Dan as he walked to the parking garage. I'd rather live in my car than give her the satisfaction of knowing about this.*

BABY SIS

"Earth to Dan!" Julie tapped on the table to get his attention. Dan glanced up at his sister sitting across the cast-iron bistro table from him. He remembers his sister bugging him all morning through a constant stream of texts and DMs until he finally agreed to meet her for coffee. However, everything else after that was a haze. *How long had he been there? What had they been talking about?*

"How's the new place?" Julie asked again as Dan started to shake off the fog.

"It's... it's great," Dan said as he tried his best to avoid eye contact with Julie. He leaned back just a bit so that the morning sun lingering behind the coconut trees released a targeted ray directly on his face. That was a perfect excuse to shield his face just enough to allow him to avoid eye contact while avoiding suspicion. She knew him well, probably better than anyone. She could always spot when he was hiding something, and that's why she had been harassing Dan for the last two weeks to meet up. She was definitely on a fact-finding mission.

Dan's sudden absence from social media raised some red flags with her a few weeks ago, and he eventually just told her that he was busy moving. He gave no details beyond that, mainly because he had none. What he thought would be a day or two's wait for an apartment to open up had taken over three weeks now. Dan couldn't bring himself to tell anyone about his struggles, so he had been sleeping in a van since moving out of the penthouse. *Officially homeless,* Dan thought. *From penthouse to living in a van under a bridge. How did I let it get to this?*

It wasn't like Dan had ever had a problem with making money. *I made a lot of money last year as an agent,* he thought, as he continued to shield his face from the sun. No, making money was not a problem. *Keeping money, now that was a different story.* Dan still didn't understand what he blew all his money on. He tried to add everything up before he moved out of the penthouse to figure out where it all went, but he was never great at keeping track of his expenses. He just spent because he knew he would have another big closing right around the corner to help pay for it. With no savings and an expense column reserved for someone that was desperately trying to keep up with the Joneses, it only took a three-month dry spell for his business to wreak havoc on his life. Money problems turned into relationship problems, which turned into a downward spiral.

Dan didn't want to talk to anyone about the breakup with Karen, so he didn't go to the office for months. Not going to the office turned into undisciplined and unproductive days, weeks, and months for his business. As an independent contractor, no one could push him to show up to work. That was one of the things that attracted Dan to real estate, the flexibility to work when you want and where you want, to "be your own boss." However, the double-edged sword of flexibility also meant he was dealing with the financial repercussions of not working, or at least not working consistently.

Dan was startled by a loud screech as Julie dragged her cast iron bistro chair to his side of the table and sat down. "There," she said with an accomplished tone. "Now you don't have to squint into the sun as you try to avoid talking to me." She looked at Dan with her patented double raised brows as if to say, "Go on, it's your turn now." Dan squirmed uncomfortably. This is why he had been avoiding Julie for the last few weeks. His entire life, Dan had told Julie everything. She was his one confidant and was always so easy to talk to. He had shared everything from dreams and ambitions to relationships and business. Julie rarely had the same interests as Dan; in fact, as she was a teacher, their worlds couldn't be more different. Maybe that's why it was always so easy to talk to Julie. They had other siblings, but he was closest with Julie, probably because they were never in direct competition with each other. She chimed in with sisterly comments and advice on occasion, but for the most part, she didn't judge him. Now Dan was struggling to keep the biggest embarrassment of his life a secret from her.

Did she already know that I was sleeping in my van? She commented on me needing a razor this morning. Did someone spot me parked by the pier at night and tell her? Was she just waiting for me to fess up? Dan wondered.

After a raised eyebrow staring contest that would have made a cowboy uncomfortable, Dan let out a defeated exhale, and his shoulders sank. "I'm staying in my van," Dan confessed. Julie's expression did not change as she stared at him and her face seemed to say, "I know." "It's only temporary," Dan continued. "I am supposed to be getting a place at the Garden Apartments next week." Julie just listened. "It was only supposed to be a couple of days, but the wait-list is not an exact science," he explained.

"Why didn't you call me?" Julie asked. "You know you can always stay in my guest room. In fact, my tenant next door is in the process of moving out as we speak. You can stay there as long as you need to."

"Baby sis as my landlord?" Dan let out with a sarcastic chuckle that was rooted more in disbelief than it was in humor. "Who would have thought?" Dan said. He had thought about asking about availability at her rental, but he couldn't bring himself to reach out. Besides, it was only two years ago that Dan had left a Sunday family get-together in frustration because he couldn't talk his sister out of buying that duplex. He knew her. There was no way she could be a landlord. And why would she even want to do that? She could put that same money into a much nicer house. What was even more frustrating was how confident she was in her decision. "I'm the real estate expert in the family. Where are you getting this ridiculous advice from?" Dan would ask her.

"I'm in a Breakfast Club," she had said with a giggle as if she were withholding a secret. "This is how I win back my Tuesdays and Wednesdays." She grinned.

"What are you talking about?" Dan asked with a look of be wilderment. Julie tried to explain further, but Dan shut the conversation down in frustration. Clearly, some other agent was trying to take advantage of his sister, and he was angry that she was so gullible. It was frustrating that she would take this stranger's advice over his. That argument stung. She had moved forward with the purchase, and a few months later she moved in, and as they often did, she called a truce by asking, "agree to disagree?" That was their way to stop any argument and realize it wasn't worth continuing the fight.

The funny thing was that it turned out she loved being a landlord. Last year she had bought another rental property and was already looking for her third rental. "Trying to be Hawaii's #1 slumlord?" Dan would often tease her. He couldn't figure out how she was affording to buy these investment properties. *She's a teacher. I know what she makes, and it is nowhere near enough to be a real estate investor. How is it that my sister, who's not even in real estate, owns more real estate than I do?* He had yet to buy his first home. When asked why he was renting, he kept saying that he was saving up to buy a mega-mansion. "Saving," he whispered under his breath, reminding himself of his failure to save anything over the last few years. No matter how much he made, he always found a way to spend to his new level of earnings.

Dan's wandering thoughts were interrupted by the waitress who stopped at their table to refill their coffee. "OK," Dan said. "I'll rent your place until I find something permanent."

"Excellent! It's settled!" Julie clapped her hands repeatedly like an overly excited cheerleader.

Julie could tell there was something else. After about a minute of silence, Dan opened his mouth to ask something but then stopped.

"Just say it!" Julie blurted out. "The suspense is killing me!"

Dan acknowledged this with a nod and then took a quick glance around to see if anyone was within listening distance. "I feel embarrassed asking you this," Dan said, "and don't get me wrong, I am proud of how you have been able to become a real estate investor..."

"But..." Julie said, encouraging Dan to finish his question.

"But I wanted to know how you could afford these properties on a teacher's salary?"

Julie smiled as if it was a question she knew he had been dying to ask for years but couldn't. She smiled as if she could finally share something with her older brother that would change his life.

"I want you to meet George," Julie said. "He runs our Breakfast Club." She paused to look at Dan and waited for a snarky comment. None followed. "It's a weekly real estate investing meet-up group. He has been my mentor through this process, and I can ask him if he would mentor you, too," Julie said with genuine excitement.

A mentor? Dan thought. He wanted to scoff at the suggestion. Dan had been a mentor in the real estate industry to a few new agents over the years, but never did he think that he needed a mentor himself. Every bone in his body felt like standing up and leaving the table. *This was clearly the guy Julie chose to take real estate advice from over her own brother.* However, something about Julie's excitement kept Dan from shutting the idea down. He nodded as if to say, "OK, you win. I'll speak with your mentor."

CHAPTER 2:

Memory Lane

Dan's phone buzzed. He glanced at it and saw it was a message from Julie. He knew it was coming, but a part of him hoped she would forget. It was the contact information for her mysterious "Mentor George" that she wanted Dan to call. A second message from Julie came through: *Hey, I just spoke with George about you and he said that he knows you! You actually used to work together a few years back. Small world. Anywayz, he's expecting your call. LMK how it goes OK?*

I used to work with him? Dan wondered as he stared at the ceiling above his bed. Finally, he sat up and glanced out the window of his new apartment. He had taken Julie up on her offer and moved into the other side of her duplex right after her tenant moved out. Not quite the ocean views that he was used to waking up to when he was living in the penthouse, but his new view of Diamond Head wasn't that bad. She had wanted to connect Dan with her mentor ever since their talk at the coffee shop last week, but he told her that he wanted to hold off until he was moved in.

"Let's wait at least until I am no longer living in my van," Dan had told her. Even last night, as they were moving furniture in, she wanted to finish early to call this "George" together. Dan pushed back. "Let me at least make it through my first night here. We can do that tomorrow."

He picked up his phone to reread the text. The phone lit up the still-dark room. *4:38 a.m.? Why is that maniac texting me at 4:38 a.m.? Why is she even up at 4:38 a.m.?* "I see how it is! I become her tenant for one day, and she immediately becomes the annoying landlord," he shouted towards the wall, hoping that his sister would hear.

He read the text again. *I used to work with him? Can you be more specific? Where did I work with him?* He began making a mental list of all the places he had worked and tried to identify which George it was. For only being in his mid-30s, Dan had quite the extensive list of previous employers. He worked at five different brokerages in the seven years he had practiced real estate. Before that, he had eleven different jobs in an eight-year span, everything from selling knives at Cutco, to grunt work at a construction site to working a desk job at an engineering firm. Dan always worked hard and did his best to excel everywhere he was, but his problem was that he got bored quickly. He was always looking for the next shiny object, greener grass, and better opportunities.

There were four or five Georges that Dan could remember working with over the years. He opened the contact that Julie sent over in a text. "First name Yoda, Last name Mentor-George." Dan let out an audible laugh. *What a goofball*, he thought.

He sent three texts to Julie back-to-back. "How do I know George? Where did I work with him? What is his last name?" He stared at his phone, waiting. "Sure, you can wake me up at 4:38 a.m. with a text, but you can't respond to mine?" Dan muttered to himself as he rolled his eyes.

"*OK, I guess I need to figure this out the old school way*," he thought. He copied the phone number, pasted it in the Google search bar, added the name George, and hit search. *Oh good, only 12,000 results*, he thought as he started to scan through the first page, looking for a familiar George. "George Davis, George Takemoto, George Owan… George Kaohiai?" *That can't be right*, Dan thought. George Kaohiai was an agent he worked with a few times at the first brokerage he ever joined as a new agent. Sure, he was a great agent, but George was not a real estate investor and certainly not a real estate investing mentor.

Dan put his phone down, sat up on his bed, and tried to recall every interaction that he'd had with this George. It'd been a few years, but Dan could clearly remember the first brokerage and office that he joined as a new real estate agent. There were many great agents there, but George was always one of the constants when Dan stopped in the office. George would be there meeting with a client or prepping to meet with a client. As a new agent, Dan opted not to sign up for a formal mentor program but ended up turning to George several times over his first few transactions for help and advice. George was always happy to answer questions and help him. Not once did he mention real estate investing to Dan though.

THE OFFICE VISIT

Later that day, Dan stopped by George's office to see if he was there, but he was out. A few familiar faces from the back of the office walked by, and when they saw Dan, they stopped to chat and catch up. It was the usual small talk that Dan had gotten great at the last few years as he worked towards top agent status. "How's business? How's the family? How about them 'Bo's?" in reference to the University of Hawaii's football team.

Then from behind him, Dan heard, "Is that Daniel-san?" Without turning around, he knew right away that it was Dwight. He was always one of the more social agents in the office and found a way to assign a nickname to everyone he met. He had been calling Dan "Daniel-san" from the first day he was introduced to the office. Dwight was obviously the class clown at every stage in his life, and even as a seasoned vet in the group, he found pleasure in making everyone chuckle with his nostalgic references and greetings. Dan didn't get that *Karate Kid* reference the first few times he heard it, so he finally decided to watch the movie on Netflix. It turned out to be a cool movie, and Dan began to wear the nickname like a badge of honor. He liked the obstacles the Karate Kid overcame. He saw himself as a Daniel Larusso type character. Maybe too confident for his own good at times, but he always found a way to come out on top.

"Who let this defector back in?" Dwight asked as he looked around with a smile, as if waiting for security to respond to his request to remove Dan from the lobby. They both laughed and caught up for a few minutes. *Wow, it felt good to laugh again*, Dan thought. *It felt good to just have actual conversations again with old friends.* After some small talk, Dan told Dwight that he was hoping to catch up with George.

"You working on a deal together?" Dwight asked.

"No, well sort of, well not really," Dan couldn't come up with the words for what he was trying to do. Did he even know what he was looking for?

"It's Wednesday, so you know George is at his second office for most of the day," Dwight said.

"That's right!" Dan said in an excited voice as he thanked Dwight, waved goodbye to everyone in the lobby, and headed towards his car.

THE 2ND OFFICE

George's second office, Dan thought. *He sure is consistent.* When Dan still worked at George's office, he noticed that on Wednesdays George wouldn't come in. Dan eventually found out that George would spend most of that day at the corner diner, Like-Like Drive Inn, and meet back-to-back there with a series of clients, agents, and prospects. Dan could remember nearly seven years ago the first time that he asked to "pick George's brain" on a few real estate business strategies, and George suggested that he meet him at that diner on Wednesday and they could discuss it. Dan thought that it was a little odd, especially since they worked in the same office. "Your brain, your rules," Dan remembered saying.

Dan went to the diner that Wednesday morning seven years ago, and in a booth with a perfect line of sight to the door sat George-- across from an older couple. *That's odd*, Dan thought. *Did he invite someone else to sit in on our meeting?*

George saw Dan and waved him in. He turned to the couple and said something that must have been related to their time ending because they got up and gathered their things to go. As Dan approached the group, George greeted him. "Dan, I want you to meet Keoki and Bev Jones. Keoki and Bev, this is Dan, a new agent who recently joined our office." They nodded with a smile. "Dan, Keoki and Bev are dear friends and clients of mine. We were just having our regular checkup," George said as he winked at the couple with a smile. They laughed and started to ask Dan about how long he had been in the business. George motioned to the group that he would be right back.

Dan thought this was strange. *Why would George leave his clients with me? Isn't he afraid that I might try to steal them?* Dan shared that he had just gotten his real estate license a few months ago. He soon learned that Keoki and Bev had been George's clients for over fifteen years and had purchased twelve properties with George so far, and were looking for their next one. *Wow*, Dan thought. *That's how George is so successful; he finds clients that need more than one property. Smart.*

George returned from settling the bill and said his farewells to the couple. They waved to Dan and then turned to the waitress and thanked her by name as if they knew her, too. George turned to Dan and motioned towards the same booth inviting him to sit down. "I'm sorry. I didn't mean to interrupt your..." Dan didn't know what to call it. "Your meeting?"

George smiled. "No apologies needed, we have an appointment, and you are right on time." George waved to someone with a smile and motioned for two coffees. It seemed like George had his own hostess and sign language here that all the waitstaff understood. George asked Dan about his background and his journey into real estate so far. Dan did his best to tell his relatively new story. He fidgeted with the rolled-up napkin around the silverware, pulling the paper seal off the wrapped package to unroll the paper napkin as he continued to smooth it out as he thought, *man, I really wish I had my coffee at this point. At least it would give my hands something to do.* Soon after, the hostess brought their coffee and took their order.

"So, pick away," George said once the hostess left.

"Huh?" Dan said, a little confused.

"You said you wanted to pick my brain on a few things...pick away," George repeated.

Dan had almost forgotten that he was the one who had asked for the meeting, and this was his show to run. Dan took a few seconds to gather his thoughts and courage. Now looking back, he wondered if he had been searching for a mentor at that first meeting.

He could still remember the awkward silence as he struggled to explain to George what he needed from that meeting seven years ago. "Here's what I think you need," George had said. "I think you need a purpose."

"What do you mean?" Dan remembered asking with a slightly concerned voice. *How does he know I needed a purpose? What would a purpose be anyway? Isn't the purpose of what we do to make money?* Dan had thought. Yet he remained quiet.

"You remind me of myself when I was just starting out in real estate," George had said. "I was ambitious and energetic and a great agent, but by my third year, I started to feel burned out and like I was making money just to make money. It turned out that I was really good at making money, but the funny thing was that money did not motivate me. It did not excite me. I got into real estate to get out of the rat race," he had said. He studied Dan's expression for signs of acknowledgment. "Although I made money at a much faster pace as I grew my real estate business, I realized that I was still very much in the rat race. Don't get me wrong, I loved being self-employed and working for myself, however I was still tied to NEEDING to work."

"You don't like to work?" Dan asked with genuine surprise in his voice. George always seemed to love what he did.

George paused, looked at Dan thoughtfully, then continued. "That's not what I said. I do love what I do. I just did not love NEEDING to work. I always felt like I was on a hamster wheel, except this time I owned the wheel and it was bigger than ever, because my expenses continued to increase as my real estate income did. I didn't see an end to the cycle on that path. It turned out that I was a rancher and not a dairy farmer," he said.

"I'm lost," Dan said. "You were a rancher as well as a real estate agent?"

"Of course not," George chuckled. "I was just running my business and my life like a cattle rancher when I should have been running it like a dairy farmer." He paused to let Dan try to figure it out. "Ranchers spend every day working to raise cattle. Then, at the end of the season, they need to sell that cattle for meat, and then they start all over again."

"What's wrong with that?" Dan asked. "I love a good steak, and without ranchers we wouldn't have steak."

"That's not the point I am getting at," George replied calmly as he continued his story. "At the end of the day, the rancher gets paid for work done, but every day he has to get up and do it again. Now compare that to a dairy farmer. Both have the job of raising cows; however, the dairy farmer keeps the cows and has a daily return as they produce milk for years versus a one-time sale of meat. I needed to set my business up like a dairy farmer, focusing on residual and passive income. So, my purpose became long-term financial security for my family instead of just income earned today. This mental shift changed the way I approached business and the way that I approached life."

Dan was way more confused than when he got there but didn't want to come off as slow, so he just nodded, hoping George would elaborate further. The rest of the meeting was a blur until George waved past Dan at the diner entrance to motion to his next coffee meeting guest. Dan glanced at his phone and couldn't believe their time was up already. He still had so many questions.

"I know we didn't cover everything you wanted to talk about today," George said as if reading Dan's mind. "I would be happy to meet with you again next Wednesday to help."

THE OFFICE MOVE

That meeting was almost seven years ago, and Dan could remember leaving the diner wishing they had more time but agreeing to come back at the same time the following Wednesday for his second meeting. He tried to recall that second meeting conversation as if he was scrolling to episode two of a new Netflix show. *Where was it? Why did I remember every detail of the first meeting but nothing about the second one? Did we have the second meeting? We scheduled it, so we must have met.*

At this point, Dan felt like he was losing his mind. He pulled up his calendar on his phone and scrolled back seven years to find that week. "When was it? Let's see, it was right after my very first closing with cousin Kimo, and that was in July!" Dan said, slowly uncovering a mystery. He could remember because he ended up having a fourth of July-themed housewarming party for Kimo right after closing. Dan scrolled to his July calendar and read through each day's appointment descriptions. There it was. "Wednesday, July 18th, coffee meeting with George," Dan read. So, meeting number two was the following Wednesday. Dan swiped through the week to read the notes, hoping he wrote about this follow-up meeting.

"Monday, review independent contractor agreement. Tuesday drop off keys, Wednesday, new office orientation." Dan couldn't believe what he was reading. He never had his follow-up meeting with George because that was the same week that he was recruited to leave that office to join a different brokerage. *Did I reschedule with George?* Dan wondered. *Did I even let him know that I couldn't make it? Or was I just a no-show?*

Dan began to dread the thought of having to reach out to someone whom he likely stood up seven years ago. *I'm sure he would understand,* Dan thought. *He knows how crazy it can be to go through a brokerage change over. Ugh, what a mistake.* He received dozens of recruiting calls within minutes of reporting his first sale closed on the MLS. Every broker or headhunter in a 25-mile radius was calling to congratulate him and in the same breath telling him that he was wasting his potential at his company. "We could help you do so much more. We have the best leads. We have the best training. We have the best technology." It was like everyone was reading from the same script. *How was I so gullible?* he wondered.

Dan got his real estate license at age twenty-nine, after he had spent most of his twenties hopping from one job to another. He had a hard time with commitment and was always chasing the greener grass. So, the flexibility and independent nature of real estate was a perfect fit for him. This was the longest he had stuck with any industry. But he hadn't yet realized how much distraction and transition there would be within the real estate industry. He spent the majority of his first four years moving from one real estate brokerage to another. "It's funny, I feel like the Lebron James of real estate," he remembered telling Julie. The first time he moved from one firm to another, he announced on Instagram that he was "Taking my talents to South Beach... I mean Waikiki Realty." That got more than a few likes, hilarious comments and memes. Everyone loved it. *Well, almost everyone*, Dan thought.

When his mom heard the news, she asked in a motherly tone, "Daniel, why did you make the change? I thought you were happy at your previous brokerage?" This told Dan that she was simultaneously curious about his decision and of the belief that he'd just made a big mistake. The fact that she called him Daniel instead of Dan, Danny, D, or one of the many other nicknames he had also indicated that she was getting ready to start a serious conversation. Dan cringed as he thought back on that talk with his mom.

"Are you kidding me? I'm a big deal. I'm highly sought after. Possibly the top free agent on the market," Dan said in his "extra-obnoxious and arrogant son with a hint of *Legally Blonde* attitude" tone to the delivery. He only brought this skill out on special occasions, to counteract his mom's Jedi mind trick questions. Under her silent, disapproving stare, Dan cleared his throat. "No, seriously, they offered me a better package, leads, and a better split than my previous company. They even paid me an upfront $15,000 sign-on bonus."

Her eyes widened. "Why would they do that?" she asked, pausing for a response. Something told Dan it wasn't his turn to speak yet. "You haven't even been licensed a year, and you have only sold one home so far. How do they know you will pan out once your family stops buying next year?" This stung a little, but it was the exact response Dan was expecting from her.

Dan's mom had always been a straight shooter with him. She knew how to support her kids' dreams and encourage them to shoot for the stars, while at the same time forcing them to stay humble and grounded. She was old school. She firmly believed that they were owed nothing and should earn everything in life. The idea of a handout from anyone always seemed to infuriate her. On many occasions Dan heard her say, "Handouts make you weak. Why would you want to become weaker? Why would I want my kids to be weak?" Dan was waiting for her to start giving him that lecture to him again, but she didn't this time. Instead, she stared through him as if she could watch the gears turning as she knew he was reciting her words in his head on his own.

In her eyes, Dan getting a "sign-on" bonus appeared to be a handout that he did not earn. *To be honest, I did feel weird when they offered me that check. I didn't ask for it*, Dan had thought. *I really didn't understand why they were offering it to me, but I would have to be an idiot not to accept free money... Right?* Dan couldn't shake his mom's Jedi lecture from his head. She didn't even give it to him this time, but after their conversation about the $15,000 signing bonus, all he could think about was her "handouts make you weak" lecture. He probably ran through their conversation about a thousand times over the next few days.

Dan eventually decided to go back and read the fine print about to the signing bonus. It turned out that it was a commission advance on his future sales, not an actual bonus. On top of that, he was committing to staying with that company for a minimum of three years. For a guy with commitment issues, this was *maika'i 'ole* (no good). Dan had picked real estate as a career largely because of his commitment issues and wanting the freedom and flexibility to do what he wanted, when he wanted. It dawned on him that he had signed a significant portion of his freedom away for the next three years by taking that "signing bonus," a handout that made him weak.

Dan realized two months after joining his new brokerage that there really wasn't anything new, different, or game-changing there, unlike his recruiter had promised. So, feeling there had been a "bait and switch," he tried to get out of his contract. He knew it would be difficult especially because he had already spent that $15,000 "bonus" on a new car within a few hours of receiving it. Dan felt stuck--like he had sold his freedom to become a voluntary hostage. It would cost him at least $15,000 to get out of his contract.

Later that year, he was recruited by another company willing to pay his $15,000 buyout from his broker and give him additional funds to get started with them. He took the deal, but that just meant he was stuck with a new company for three years.

This cycle continued through five different brokerages over his first four years, and he eventually found himself committed to staying with his fifth brokerage, now owing them $45,000 for a three-year period. He was just over two years into that commitment when the exhaustion of all that moving around caught up with him. Every time he made a move, he thought he was jumping into greener grass and more opportunities, but it usually set him back by at least six months because he kept having to learn new systems and new office procedures in addition to focusing on growing his business.

Promises were made and promises were broken at each stop, but one thing Dan did learn throughout his moves, was that he needed to take responsibility for his own success. Eventually, he decided to start paying for his own Zillow and Realtor.com leads, and it turned out that he had a knack for converting online leads into clients. Over the next few years, he used these sites as his primary lead sources and kept increasing his ad and lead generation spending budget. Each year for the past four years, he had been a top producer and in the running for the top individual agent spot in each office that he was in. It became simple math for Dan: the more he spent on leads, the more clients and closings he would get. At the peak last year, he spent over $85,000 on online lead generation.

Dan's financial problems started when the cost of those leads nearly doubled overnight. There had been incremental price increases over the last few years, as to be expected, but this was a significant jump. He would either need to double his ad spend or decrease his online footprint by 50%, which would lead to a 50% reduction in his business the following year. *Did the numbers even make sense anymore?* Dan remembered thinking as he tried to create a spreadsheet that accurately represented his new cost of doing business. And what other option did he have?

Several months into this new cost structure, Dan knew he was in trouble. His costs were up drastically, and his lead flow was down. His already thin margins were being slashed on both ends. How long could his business last on these numbers? How long could *he* last? Dan was never one to have any sort of business re-serves. He made money, and he spent money. That was the cycle. It seemed to always work in his favor because he was always able to make money. Then just like that, in January of this year, with a decreased deal flow and no real prospects in the pipeline, Dan had to decide between paying for leads and paying his rent. It took him over two weeks to cancel the leads because he was tied into long-term contracts. He finally had to cancel his credit card so that the payments didn't go through. Chances were, even if he didn't, the charges would have been declined because his cards had been maxed out for a while now.

With no credit, no immediate prospects and no reserves, Dan was only able to make a partial rent payment in March. He asked the landlord for an extension, which was granted. However, that extension came and went, and he still couldn't make rent. So the landlord delivered an official notice to pay or quit, which started the eviction process.

CHAPTER 3:

The 2nd Meeting

Dan pulled up to the restaurant. "Like-Like Drive Inn," Dan said out loud with a nostalgic tone. It had been a while since he was last there. It was only a few blocks from Dan's office and was on the corner of Kanunu and Ke'eaumoku Street, so he passed by it often and whenever he went to the mall. However, Dan had not stopped there since... That feeling of dread crept back. *Since my first meeting with George almost seven years ago,* he thought. Dan still couldn't believe that he stood George up and now he was there hoping to just walk in and say hi.

He got out of the car and closed the door. He only took a few steps towards the entrance before he could see George inside, standing next to his usual booth chatting with someone. Dan couldn't tell if his guest was just getting there or just getting ready to leave. In either case, he was impressed with George's consistency. It was 10:45 a.m., and Dan remembered that George ended every meeting on the 45s. That gave him enough time to prep for his next appointment, which usually started on the hour.

He started to fidget with his keys and opened his car door again - not to get back inside, but to pretend that he had forgotten something. This allowed him to peer through the car door and into the restaurant without looking like a complete stalker. But all he could see was the cash register and hostess. *There she is,* Dan thought as he saw George's guest walk by and thank the hostess.

He closed his door again and started to head in. He smiled and nodded at George's previous guest as she walked out, and he walked in. He looked up and saw George back at his booth pulling out his laptop. *OK, how do I play this?* Dan thought as he ran a few scenarios in his head. *Is this a chance encounter? Do I come out and tell George that I came here looking for him?*

He motioned to the hostess that he was going to see George, and she nodded. Seven years later, and nearly nothing had changed. George sat in the burgundy diner booth that might as well have had his name on it. The wood-patterned countertop blended into the wood-paneled dividing wall against which George was sitting, in a very familiar-looking Aloha shirt. He had two or three favorite shirts that he wore on rotation. *Some things never change*, Dan thought. He still could not believe that this was Julie's mentor.

"George," Dan called out a few feet before he got to his booth. George looked up.

"Dan Carter," he said with a smile as he slid out of his booth to greet Dan. "How have you been?" George asked.

"Great," Dan said. "I had a record year last year and am hoping for an even better one this year." The moment he said that, Dan felt the shame of the lie and wanted to change the topic. It had become almost automatic for Dan to sneak his sales credentials into every small talk scenario. That had been his go-to phrase for the last few years. It was always true, to an extent, but now...

"Julie told me you may be calling," George said.

That caught Dan off guard. *How much did she tell George?* "Sorry, I didn't mean to interrupt you. I just wanted to say hi. You probably need to prep for your next client meeting," he stammered, trying to find the right response.

"Nonsense," George replied. "Have a seat. I have a 45-minute break before my next appointment. Let's chat now."

Dan was not ready to have an entire conversation with George. He was hoping to just reconnect today so that it wouldn't be awkward when he called him to pick his brain in a couple of weeks. *I guess this is happening now*, he thought as he slid into the same booth he sat in seven years ago. George motioned to the waitress for two coffees.

"If I remember correctly, you and I had a conversation here a few years ago," George said.

Dan was surprised that George would remember that. *He must meet hundreds of people in this booth every year. Does he also remember that I stood him up for our second meeting?*

"Well?" George asked.

"Well, what?" Dan asked with an awkward smile.

"Are you a rancher or a dairy farmer?" George asked with a smile. It was like they had picked up the same conversation from seven years ago.

Dan laughed. "I never did quite get what you meant by that. That's one of the reasons I wanted to reconnect with you. That, and Julie wants me to ask about... Something about your Breakfast Club?" Dan said with an unsure tone.

George leaned back a little, as if trying to size up Dan. He retreated into the left corner of his booth, propping his chin up against his left fist, seeming to get ready to take a break from their conversation and get lost in deep thought.

Dan shifted as the silence was starting to get uncomfortable.

"How much do you know about the Breakfast Club?" George asked in a tone that signaled to Dan that this was the first of several questions in a list.

"Not much. Julie just said that you meet weekly and talk about investing. Basically, a real estate investor meet-up," Dan replied.

"Yes, and no," George said. "Yes, we meet weekly and talk about investing. But no, it's not a real estate investor meet up. It's an exclusive club with limited members, and we have one focus and one goal," George paused to see if Dan was tracking.

"Let me guess! Make money?" Dan said with a chuckle.

"We do indeed talk about making money in this group, but that is not the focus. The focus is freedom," George paused again. This time Dan remained silent to let George continue. "Financial freedom to choose. Freedom to do things because we want to and not because we NEED to. Freedom to choose how we spend our time," George said this staring off into the center of the diner as if reading his investor club's motto from the back wall with pride. "Most people think that they need more money, so they decide to work harder, or get another job, continue to climb the corporate ladder. But when they get there, when they land that higher paying job, when they have a record year in real estate sales, they are just as unsatisfied as they were in their previous position. Most people work their whole lives chasing money, only to find out at the end that they were chasing freedom and never actually got there."

"Are you saying we don't need money?" Dan asked, somewhat surprised at the direction this conversation was heading.

"Not quite," George said. "It's just that our relationship with money is off. Rather than a life centered around pursuing money, which rarely results in sustained happiness, we would be much better off living a life focused on the pursuit of freedom. Financial freedom, freedom of choice, and freedom of time can all lead to sustained happiness."

"And money?" Dan asked.

"And money," George said, "Money, or rather the 'flow of money' is just a tool used to help us achieve those freedoms." He looked at Dan, who was now sitting back in his booth staring past George towards the middle of the diner, trying to visually track everything that George just said.

Dan had a question; he just couldn't articulate it. He gathered his thoughts and focused back on George.

"I have been in a position where I," Dan paused, thinking through his word choices carefully, "where I had money. Lots of it. And I have been in a position where I had no money. And from what I can tell, I am happiest when I have money," Dan said, looking at George.

"Of course," George said with a smile. "That is usually the case and is to be expected. But did this happiness last?"

"No, but that's only because the money didn't..." Dan stopped short of completing his thought, realizing that he had just given away the fact that he had money problems.

WEALTH MEASURED IN TIME

"Most people think that the key to being rich is making more money," George said.

"It's not?" Dan asked, confused.

"Dan, you had a great year in real estate last year," George said.

"Yes, um, thank you. It was..." Dan sat up a little straighter and prepped himself to move on to a much more comfortable topic: his success in real estate.

George jumped back in as if trying to steer a ship back on course and continued with the second part of his thought. "From what I can tell, you sold nearly $20 million in real estate last year. That is very impressive. My guess is that you made a lot more money last year than you did when you started seven years ago, correct?"

"Of course," Dan said with a laugh. "Way more. When I got started, I barely had enough to survive for a few months. I had to hustle to get my first deal closed so that they wouldn't shut off my MLS subscription for non-payment." *Things were a struggle back then, but they also seemed so much simpler,* he thought.

"Excellent. I knew you would be a great agent. Great agents like you are always looking to increase their business year after year, and as a result make more money year after year. However, my question to you is, would you say that you are working towards increasing your wealth?"

It felt like a trick question to Dan, but the obvious answer was yes, so he nodded in agreement.

"What if I told you that wealth was not defined by money, rather it was defined by time?" George paused to gauge Dan's facial expression as it would help him decide how much more he was going to share with him today.

Dan started to feel like this was a red pill versus blue pill moment unfolding before him, and George was playing the role of Morpheus from the Matrix, doing his best to explain a concept that had no bearing within the parameters of Dan's current reality.

"Robert Kiyosaki details this concept in *The Cash-flow Quadrant.* It is a must-read book that could change your life." George paused. "You see that cashier?" George asked. "He probably takes home about $3,000-$4,000 a month. My guess is that his living expenses are also close to $3,000-$4,000 a month. He's likely breaking even, living paycheck to paycheck as most hard-working Americans do. Now, if he lost his job and all his active income stopped, his defined wealth would be how long his existing assets, like savings in the bank and retirement accounts, would last to pay for his existing liabilities and bills. So, if he has $10,000 in the bank, and it costs him $3,000-$4,000 a month to live, his wealth at the moment equals two to three months. Does that make sense?"

Dan had never heard of wealth defined in this way, but it made sense to him.

"So, now that you know my definition of wealth, let me ask you a question. Are you wealthier now than you were seven years ago?" George asked in a slightly quieter tone, knowing that it was a sensitive question.

Dan could not believe what he was being asked. *How dare he! How much did Julie tell George about his situation?* He could feel himself getting angry. *You are not supposed to talk about these kinds of things with just anyone. These are reserved for closed-door conversations with your accountant. Who does this guy think he is?* Thoughts were racing through Dan's head as he searched for a way to cut their conversation short.

"Now, I don't know anything about your situation," George said, "but if you are anything like the average hard-working American, if you are anything like I was as a young go-getter real estate agent in my first few years," he paused as if to check Dan's temperature, "I made a lot of money in real estate and was probably on a very similar trajectory as you are on now. I won every award you could think of at my company and from our local Realtors association, but as my income grew each year, my expenses grew proportionately. I always found a way to spend just more than I would make that year. Although my sales were consistent, my lifestyle was partially supported by credit card debt."

Dan could feel himself start to calm down as George explained further.

"I was on a quest to earn as much money that was humanly possible for me, but I could start to feel the burnout. I felt like I needed to earn more every year just to keep up with my lifestyle," George said. "I spent a lot of time thinking about leaving real estate. But then what? I didn't have enough money saved to last more than a few months, let alone a lifetime if I wanted to retire. Would I just start all over in another industry? It would be like finally getting off of one hamster wheel and hopping right on a shiny new hamster wheel. Where did it end? How did it end? By sheer luck, a client gave me a gift after I helped him buy his third rental property. It was the book *Rich Dad, Poor Dad* and a board game called *CA$HFLOW 101*, both by Robert Kiyosaki," George said.

Dan had a copy of that book. Julie gave it to him a few years ago for his birthday. He never read it. Dan wasn't a big reader. He always felt he should read more but never quite understood how people found the time. He was always working.

"Reading that book changed my life," George said. "Playing that game opened up new worlds of opportunity for me. I learned things over a few weeks of playing it that proved far more important than almost all of my previous education combined."

"From a game?"

George nodded. "It is the only reason that I am financially free today."

Dan felt the same level of awkwardness or embarrassment that he had felt when George asked about Dan's wealth, or lack thereof.

Normal people do not discuss personal finances, Dan thought. But he was very curious about what George really meant by being financially free.

As if reading Dan's mind, George expounded on cue. "I have been able to acquire enough passive income and cash-flowing assets to far exceed my expenses. So even though I don't have all the money in my account today, if I chose to never work or never close another sale, or earn any sort of active income again, my passive income would continue to come in and pay for all of my expenses."

"So why are you still working?" Dan asked, trying to hide a hint of skepticism in his voice.

"Ah, great question. That's where the magic is," George said with a smile. "Once I figured out a plan to help me achieve financial freedom, that became my new obsession. The burnout that I felt before? Gone! I had a whole new motivation. I was determined to work harder than I had ever worked in my life, and in five years I would be financially free. I could walk away and never have to work again," George said, his eyes lighting up like he was telling his favorite story. "My business continued to thrive. I stuck to my cash-flow plan, and I hit my financial freedom number in just under four years. That was nearly twelve years ago. The moment I hit my financial freedom number, the thought of stopping just didn't appeal to me anymore. I continued to work, and not because I had to. It was because I wanted to. I felt such freedom, and everything became so much easier. Life became easier, business became easier. It turns out that the weight and stress of the unknown, and the financial pressures that I had, were the reasons I was feeling burned out, not the actual work itself. I love what I do. Not only that... I wanted to shout from the rooftops to share with my friends, my family, my clients, and my colleagues the magic of this financial freedom path. My business has since shifted to nearly a hundred percent focus on investment real estate to help people achieve financial freedom first, and then generational wealth next."

George looked up and saw the cloud of questions on Dan's face. "I apologize," he said. "I tend to get carried away and go on tangents when I get excited. You have questions, and I would be happy to answer them, but you'll have to promise to show up to our next appointment." And with a simple raise of an eyebrow George let Dan know that he remembered being stood up for their second meeting nearly seven years ago.

CHAPTER 4:

The Cash-Flow Breakfast Club

It felt weird for Dan to be walking through his old office training room again. He was early for the meet-up group that George asked him to attend. It was almost seven, so most of the usual agents and staff were done for the day, but he did see a few familiar faces and said hello as they were leaving. He strolled through the room as one might do at an art exhibit, looking at the agent banners displayed throughout. There were a lot of faces that he remembered from seven years ago—perhaps more than he knew at his current brokerage.

Dan took a seat at the very back of the training room, hoping to blend into the wall as he observed George's meeting. "The Cash-flow Breakfast Club," he said to himself, appreciating the irony of a Breakfast Club meeting at seven in the evening.

He heard a cheerful squeal from across the room. It was Julie, and she immediately made her way to the back to sit with Dan. She squeezed her brother's hand tightly and gave him an excited side hug. Dan smiled at his sister, but his eyes pleaded, *don't embarrass me!*

Dan tried to show no emotion but surprised himself by how excited he was to be there. There was an energy around him that he hadn't felt in a while. The room soon filled up, and he saw George at the front engaged in a conversation with a gentleman who looked to be in his seventies.

"That's Sam," Julie whispered. "Rumor has it that he will be ringing the gong today! Once you reach your financial freedom number you get to ring the gong."

George asked everyone to take their seat.

The gong rang. Cheers and applause continued for what seemed like forever as Sam bowed and waved to the group pretending to be a star performer taking a bow at the end of a play. Finally, he cleared his throat and motioned for them to let him speak. "I remember joining this group a little over five years ago. I was sixty-five then, and as you all know, I worked hard all my life but found myself in a position where I couldn't retire." He cleared his throat again, clearly not comfortable with all the attention. He glanced over at George with a look that said, "Do I have to do this?" George smiled and nodded, giving Sam a boost of encouragement to continue.

"I worked all my life making a decent living in hospitality management. I'm currently a hotel manager at the Outrigger in Waikiki, a job that I worked hard to get over many years of dedication to my company. I made a great income. Unfortunately, I never put much effort into learning about retirement, so I did what my HR director and company-referred financial planner told me to do when I was hired almost thirty-five years ago. 'Just allocate a percentage of your paycheck to your retirement every month and forget about it. You don't want to play that game where you live and die with every up and down of the stock market,' the HR director told me. That sounded good to me," Sam shared. At this point, he was staring off to the corner of the conference room like he was watching it unfold before his eyes again, yearning to tell his younger self to wake up and pay attention. "I took the easy way out of planning for my future and bought into the 'set it and forget it' mindset of retirement investing. 'On average, the market has increased by ten percent a year for nearly the last century!'" he exclaimed, mimicking the villain of his story: his financial planner. "That's not investment advice; that's a sales pitch!" Sure, that advice makes sense if you have ninety years. It even makes sense if you have 30 years... But what happens when you are one year away from your planned retirement, and the market crashes, and you lose fifty percent of your retirement nest egg?"

Waiting until it averaged back out over the next thirty years was not really an option for Sam at age sixty-five. That's what forced him to take his retirement into his own hands. He started by educating himself on real estate investing options for retirement. He became obsessed with the Bigger Pockets podcast and various YouTube investor coaches who helped him with his knowledge, but ultimately, he didn't have the confidence to get started on his own without a coach or a mentor. That path took him down a rabbit hole and into the "dark side" of the real estate investing world. It was the side that monetized the education and mentorship of new wannabe investors.

"Every Tom, Dick, and Harry who found themself on HGTV also ended up creating a paid investor seminar series. I'm all for paying for a good education," Sam said, "but once it got to the point where I was $38,000 into a real estate investor education program, and when I finally reached what I thought would be the end of the course, where they would give me the good stuff and next steps to start investing, it turned out that they'd withheld the best stuff for a separate, 'advanced' course, and that would cost me another $35,000! Don't get me wrong, there was great information in the course, but it wasn't leading me down a path of real estate investing. It was leading me down a path of feeling like I needed to spend more money on investor education. I didn't know when it would end. It wasn't until I reached out to George for help that I finally saw a clear path to retirement. George," Sam said, turning to him, "I truly appreciate what you have done for me and my family."

Sam turned back to the room. "Over the years, George helped me buy and sell several homes as my family moved from one neighborhood to another, but we never discussed real estate investing. I reached out to George five years ago because I felt I would have to sell my home to try to dig myself out of the hole I was in. At first, I didn't want to open up and share all my issues and concerns with him. I was both frustrated and embarrassed by the entire situation, and I... I just didn't want to talk about it. I don't remember exactly what George said to get me to open up, but he's good at that. He tends to know what to say to bring something out of you that you didn't know you wanted or even needed to get out. It was at one of George's famous coffee networking meetings that I opened up to him." The crowd laughed. "Oh, you've been to one of those, too?" Sam asked the group with a smile.

From the reactions seen around the room, it appeared that everyone there had had at least one coffee meeting with George at his "second office."

Industrywide, George was famous for these meetings. Sometimes he would be at Like-Like Drive Inn for several hours straight as he would say bye to one client and welcome the next a few minutes later, often lining up two to three coffee meetings back-to-back. If you showed up early, he would wave you into his usual booth and introduce you to his previous guest as he would get up to pay for the bill and take a restroom break. Dan couldn't help but think how strategic and brilliant this move was. You, a future client, got to engage in small talk with someone that you just met, another client of George. Those conversations would always turn to how you both think George is amazing. *This guy is a true Jedi master when it comes to real estate. And here I am sitting in a room full of his Jedi mentees*, Dan thought. *Is it possible that a hotel manager knows more about real estate than I do?* Dan's internal dialog started to take over, and he drifted off into his main place of comfort as of late, a space of self-pity, mixed with equal parts sadness and anger.

PIFL: PASSIVE INCOME FOR LIFE

The crowd broke out in laughter again, which snapped Dan back to the present. He didn't hear what Sam said, but he could tell it was a joke at George's expense by the way that George was clapping his hands in amusement. "Now, five years later, after following each step of the snowball investing plan that George created for me, we have achieved the PIFL needed to retire. We are financially free."

Dan turned to Julie and mouthed, "PIFL? What's PIFL?"

She tore out a page from her notebook, jotted down a message, folded the paper up and slid it to Dan like passing a note in class. It read, "Passive Income For Life." Dan stared at the page, then watched Sam wrap up his speech.

Passive income was not a foreign concept to Dan. It was all the rage in the real estate industry. Dan had received passive income checks a few times because someone he helped recruit to his office sold a home and he got a cut of their sales, but the checks were usually only for a few hundred dollars. For a few years, he put a good amount of effort into recruiting agents to his brokerage so that he could cash in on this passive income craze. It was nice to receive money that he did not actively work for. This was sold to him as the retirement income that could support him when he was ready to step away from actively selling real estate. However, Dan eventually started seeing it as the great pyramid scheme of real estate. Many companies had a form of this, and they were all flawed, because the passive income depended on the agents you recruited actually staying with the company and actually selling real estate long-term. But the reality was that most agents moved from brokerage to brokerage every few years. Although it was nice to receive random passive income checks occasionally, he saw that this was by no means a long-term income source that would support him when he retired. Any effort put into recruiting only provided short-lived results, usually for one to two years before the agent either moved on to another brokerage or slowly wound down and stopped selling real estate altogether.

Dan looked down at the explanation that Julie had written for him: "Passive Income For Life." He circled the "For Life" and drew a big question mark by it, then gave the note back to Julie. "Ask George about the shark," Julie wrote, ending her note with a smiley face.

George held up a check in a picture frame so everyone could see. He then walked over to Sam and presented it to him as if it were his graduate certificate. Another outbreak of applause from the group. Dan glanced at Julie quizzically. "Cost of the program," Julie whispered.

Dan nodded and turned back to watch the presentation. *Of course, there was a cost. But why was Sam getting a check and not the other way around?*

Sam looked at the check, chuckled, and held it up like a trophy he had just won. George shook Sam's hand and gave him another nod of approval before turning his attention back to the group. "Okay! Who will be ringing the gong next?"

Eight or nine hands shot up, one of which was Julie's. She was like a kid in the classroom, excited to share a story and hoping the teacher called on her. George pointed to someone in the front row. "How many more doors do you need?" He asked.

Dan leaned over to see who George was pointing at. He knew that person. It was Leilani, a real estate agent in George's office. Dan recalled a few conversations he had with her when he was in that office as well, and if he remembered correctly, she was a part-time agent. She mostly worked on the weekends because she was a single mom and had another full-time job.

"I only need three more doors," Leilani announced proudly.

"How exciting!" George replied. "Would you mind breaking down your core numbers for the group?"

She stepped over to the whiteboard and wrote "Leilani's Core Numbers," then listed several bullet points. She turned to the group to read off her list. "I've been working the system for four years. The first two were the hardest, but once I got rid of my housing expense it became much easier. Now, my financial freedom number is $6,525 a month." She pointed to the next bullet point. "I now own eleven doors. Each door has an average PIFL of $475 a month." Julie nudged Dan to get him to acknowledge that she had taught him the meaning of PIFL. Dan rolled his eyes. "So, my PIFL deficit is $1,300 a month, which breaks down to just under three more doors." She circled "3 more doors" several times, and underlined it with excitement. "I have a duplex under contract right now. So, if everything goes as planned, I will be looking for my last door by the end of the year." Everyone gave her a round of applause.

Leilani's Core Numbers

- Financial freedom number = $6,525 a month
- Doors Owned = 11
- Average PIFL per door = $475
- Total PIFL = $5,225
- PIFL Deficit = $1,300
- Additional doors needed for financial freedom = 3

"Thank you for sharing, Leilani. We are all so proud of you," George said as he watched her take her seat. He turned back to the group. "OK, Leilani will be ringing the gong in about 11 months. Anyone plan to ring it sooner?"

Two hands shot up again, and Julie's was one of them. Dan didn't even recognize her. There was no way his sister was rich and ready to retire. He saw where she had been living the last few years. It was no mansion.

George pointed to Julie and nodded, letting her know that it was her turn to share.

"My PIFL deficit is about $3,000 per month, and I am under contract right now to purchase a 10-unit apartment building on the east coast that has a positive cash-flow, I mean, PIFL of $3,209," Julie said with a smile. I have a 90-day due diligence period. So, I should be getting my first PIFL check and ringing the gong in about four months!" Julie was beaming as the group gave her a round of applause.

"The butter mochi countdown has officially started," George announced to the group and they all laughed. Julie was famous for her butter mochi, and when announcing her goals to the group a few years ago, she promised to bring a pan in for everyone in the group when she hit her numbers and rang the gong.

The rest of the session was a blur for Dan. His head was spinning, and he had a hard time focusing on any of the discussion topics that George was detailing on the whiteboard after that. He kept trying to figure out how his sister, the teacher, had more money than him. How was she about to become financially free while he was drowning in debt?

Once the meeting ended, Dan slipped out the back. He texted Julie to say he had a client meeting. That was a lie. He just needed to clear his head and try to grasp what he had just experienced. It felt like a different dimension had opened up, and he was still trying to figure out if it was real. He knew George would ask him what he thought, and Dan was not ready to answer that. He did not know what to think yet. He still had so many questions and doubts.

CHAPTER 5:

Winning Back Tuesdays and Wednesdays

The following morning Dan was both excited and nervous as he drove back to meet George at his office. He had sent George a text after the meet-up to thank him and apologize for leaving without saying goodbye. He also asked what the cost would be to join the group and hire George as a coach. George replied that he would be willing to meet first thing the next morning to discuss that and to answer all of Dan's questions about the Breakfast Club.

Must be expensive, Dan thought. He felt conflicted. He knew there would be a cost to a program like this. But if it could help him achieve results like Sam's or what his sister was apparently about to achieve, what dollar amount would he be willing to pay for that? "Ugh! Who am I kidding? No matter the cost, I don't have the money right now. My credit cards are maxed out, and I am barely treading water. I really need to get my active income back on track before I can even start to think of passive income."

He stepped out of the car and walked to the entrance of George's office. "Don't sign anything. Don't commit to anything," he whispered under his breath in preparation for the hard sales pitch that he felt would be coming his way.

As Dan entered the lobby, the agent manning the front desk greeted him with a smile. Dan explained he was there to see George. "Of course. Follow me," the agent said, then he guided Dan past the lobby and training room, back to the private offices. He stopped at George's office, knocked, and poked his head in to announce that Dan was there to see him. George appeared to be deep in thought, solving some sort of math problem on a spreadsheet. When he noticed Dan he smiled and motioned for him to pull up a chair.

"Let me just finish this one thing," George said.

"Take your time. I'm a few minutes early," Dan said as he took a seat in one of the three empty chairs.

This didn't look like a traditional top producer office, Dan thought. He had looked George up on Homesnap last night and saw that he had more sales than Dan did the previous year. Significantly more. Yet, there wasn't a single award or certificate displayed on the wall. Dan noticed a pile of Top Producer certificates neatly stacked in the corner of his office. How this contrasted with his own office! He usually had to rearrange his wall every year to ensure that his most recent award was displayed front and center, at eye level, and everything else cascaded out from there.

George's walls were covered with frames, but they weren't certificates. Dan tried to focus in on the frames on the left wall that was across from him. He stood up to get a closer look and realized that they were all checks. He started to read through them. They were all $10,000 checks. *Was that the cost of the program?* Dan wondered. But then he noticed that each $10,000 check was made out to a different organization, with many being political groups. Some were companies, and a few were written out to big organizations like the NRA and PETA. *Very strange,* Dan thought as he continued to browse the wall.

He turned his attention to the opposite wall, where the frames contained color-coded spreadsheets with what looked like P&L breakdowns of various rental properties. On that same wall was a black, glass dry erase board that spanned nearly floor to ceiling, with over a hundred names written on it in blue marker. Next to each name, there was a column heading that said "FF#." Underneath that heading, next to everyone's name, was a dollar amount between $3,800 and $25,000 a month. The next column heading was "Doors owned." Those numbers ranged from 0 to 427. The next column heading was "Current PIFL," after which Dan saw "PIFL Deficit/Surplus." The last three columns were "Start Date," "Gong Date," and "Check returned Y/N?" Dan was struggling to piece all the information together.

Based on Sam's speech last night, Dan gathered that the "Gong Date" meant someone rang the gong once they hit their financial freedom number and could retire. Glancing down the list of all the people who had successfully rung the gong, Dan recognized many of the names. They were not all George's clients. Many, if not most of these names were agents in George's office. "Pete?" Dan said to himself. "Pete rang the gong?" Pete was a new agent just starting in the office as Dan was leaving for his subsequent brokerage. From what Dan could tell, Pete was quiet, and a part-time agent who only did a handful of deals a year. *How the hell is Pete better off than me?*

Member	FF#	Doors Owned	Current PIFL	PIFL Deficit	Start Date	Gong Date	Check Returned?
Billy	$138k	12	$51k	$87k	2/19		
Seth	$97k	19	$112k	$0	4/18	9/21	Yes
Ramzi	$175k	19	$104k	$71k	11/20		
Micah	$214k	23	$145k	$69k	9/18		
Leilani	$73k	11	$63k	$10k	3/17		
Elna	$140k	8	$52k	$88k	5/20		
Amy	$190k	15	$86k	$104k	12/18		
Sam	$130k	14	$132k	$0	4/16	2/21	Yes
Pete	$45k	5	$57k	$0	5/14	5/19	Yes
Sarah	$60k	12	$35k	$25k	7/18		
Brooke	$300k	47	$317k	$0	5/06	7/12	Yes
Austen	$45k	6	[illegible]	$173k	[illegible]		

George was still typing away at his laptop, so Dan took a seat again and began to observe some artwork hanging on the right wall. The most prominent piece was a three feet wide framed picture of Kobe Bryant drenched in sweat, in the middle of a game, walking and staring down the camera with a fierce intensity. The quote on the poster read, "I CAN'T RELATE TO LAZY PEOPLE. WE DON'T SPEAK THE SAME LANGUAGE. I DON'T UNDERSTAND YOU. I DON'T WANT TO UNDERSTAND YOU. - KOBE BRYANT."

Dan got chills. "What a beast!" he said out loud. George looked up at Dan and turned his chair.

"Big Kobe fan?" Dan asked, pointing to the picture.

"I've never met Kobe Bryant in person," George said, "but I have learned a lot from him. In his prime, he made everything look so effortless. It was like he was playing a completely different game than his competition. However, everything that you read about Kobe tells a completely opposite story. He worked harder than everyone else. He was more focused than everyone else. He put in the work every morning before most people even woke up. That drive is what enabled him to excel seemingly effortlessly once it was game time. Just like being a successful real estate agent or real estate investor, it's the focus and the work that you put in behind the scenes that will eventually lead to your success when the lights are on."

Dan nodded and smiled. He loved sports analogies. It was one of the first things that George said that he could fully understand and relate to.

"Well, you didn't come here to talk sports. So, what did you think about last night?"

"I... I don't even know where to start. How much is the program, I guess, is my main question," he said in a slightly uncomfortable tone.

"Great question," George replied. "Before we talk price, do you have any idea what you would actually be paying for?"

"Weekly classes and a spreadsheet?" Dan replied with a smirk and a smile to let George know it was a joke.

George chuckled. "Yes, that is exactly it, weekly meetings and a spreadsheet," he replied. "People come to me when they realize they are no longer happy with their status quo. They are not happy with their current financial situation or the path that they have been on. The point of working, the point of earning an income, is to support our lives, families, passions, dreams, and to eventually get to the point where we no longer need to work. Unfortunately, most people work their entire lives, barely present for their families, never pursuing their passions and deferring their dreams. The average American does not have a clear path to financial freedom. They will likely have to work their entire lives until they physically can't do so anymore, and then at that point, they will have to rely on their family, the government or both to support them. It's a sad cycle," George said as he looked at Dan, who was slowly nodding his head.

"Debt and financial obligations are the number one stressors holding the majority of people captive. I care about one thing, and that is freedom. Financial freedom. If I could help people achieve this one thing then they would have the freedom to do what they want. They would have the freedom to spend more time with family if they wanted to. They would have the freedom to pursue their passions if they wanted to. They would have the freedom to dream bigger because they would no longer have the stress of their financial obligations tethering them to their captive reality. I don't help people buy real estate. I don't help people invest in real estate," George said, and paused as he knew that would raise questions from Dan. "I only focus on, and I only care about helping my clients achieve financial freedom. If someone wants me to help them buy, sell or rent a home, I will only do it if it is part of a structured plan towards their financial freedom. If an agent wants me to mentor them and help them grow their business or become a real estate investor, I will only do it if it is a key element in helping that agent achieve financial freedom."

Dan raised his finger like a student hoping to interrupt the professor. "How do you or they know what is and what is not a step towards their financial freedom?" Dan asked.

George smiled as if he was happy that Dan asked the exact question he was supposed to at that time. "Dan, I asked you this question at the diner when we met, and I could tell you were offended."

Dan remembered the talk about money that caught him off guard.

"Are you okay if we pick up where we left off? Even if it is uncomfortable?"

Dan nodded.

"Okay, Dan, based on your sales, I see that you sold significantly more homes last year than you did your first year in real estate. It is safe to assume that you made significantly more money last year compared to your first year in real estate." It wasn't phrased as a question, but George looked at Dan for a visual cue of acknowledgment, which he received. "Dan, anything you share here does not leave this room. So, remembering our conversation on wealth being measured in time... Are you wealthier now," he paused again, "than you were when you started seven years ago?"

Every fiber in Dan's body wanted to say yes. His pride, his ego needed him to say yes. But he couldn't. He shook his head and let out an exhale. It was almost as if at that moment, he was admitting that he had a problem, and by acknowledging it, he felt like he could now actually do something about it.

"Most agents, most people really, are in the same boat as you," George said in a reassuring tone. "It is our education and our society as a whole that puts us in this position. Society tells us that we need to wear our financial status on our sleeves, that our houses, cars, and clothes, should reflect our financial status. As a result, our lifestyles almost always expand to, and often beyond, the level of our earnings. In my first year in real estate, I made $38,000. It wasn't a lot, but guess what? I survived. I didn't have much in the bank after bills, but I survived. In year three in the business, I was a go-getter. I made $157,000 in real estate! But guess what? The cost of my house, cars, clothes, and lifestyle increased rapidly. Even though it paid the bills, at the end of the day I still had almost nothing in savings. I realized that even though I had complete control over my income, I was still very much in the rat race. Most people feel that they have an income problem. 'If I only made more money, my problems would be solved.' In reality, most people have a spending problem, not an income problem. Don't get me wrong, income is still a critical piece of the puzzle. However, it is not how much income you make, rather it is what kind of income you make that matters the most."

ACTIVE INCOME VS. PASSIVE INCOME

George stood up and walked behind Dan to an open space on the whiteboard. He wrote on the board, "Active Income vs. Passive Income."

"Some people like to call it vertical income vs. horizontal income," George added. He drew a vertical line under the active income heading, and he drew a horizontal line under the passive income heading. "Imagine that you are at the bottom of this vertical line," George said, circling the bottom of the line and drawing a stick figure holding a boulder over his head. "This is you. This is everyone working hard to increase their active income. This income is earned in bursts. The harder you work, the longer you work, the higher you lift this vertical line, the more money you can make, which is great," George said as he looked back at Dan. "The problem with active or vertical income is the moment you stop pushing, the moment you lose focus, the moment you slow down or stop working, your income comes back down or stops altogether. Active (or vertical) income always ends at zero."

He moved over to the horizontal line and drew a stick figure pushing a boulder at the beginning of the line down a slight decline. "There is work involved in setting up a horizontal stream of income, but once it is set up, and you push, it just keeps going. We call that PIFL, or Passive Income For Life." George wrote "PIFL" next to the horizontal line. "The problem is that most horizontal income streams are not enough to replace active income or to retire from. That is where the snowball, or stacking process, comes into play. If you could strategically stack several horizontal streams of income on top of each other, you can eventually hit any number that you need to." George drew several horizontal lines, one on top of the other until it matched the height of the vertical line.

Dan studied the whiteboard, then picked up one of the pens. "What if this isn't enough?" he said as he circled the lowest horizontal line on the chart. "This sounds great, but you need money to invest in real estate and buy these rental properties and from what it looks like, it will take many years until someone will have enough horizontal income to even make a dent in their expenses. So how does someone who is living paycheck to paycheck save up enough to buy all these horizontal lines?" Dan asked.

Without skipping a beat, George picked up the eraser, cleared a section on the board, and started another diagram. At the top, he wrote *Weekly Income Breakdown: $1,000 a week* as the main heading. Then under that, he wrote out *Mon ($200), Tues ($200), Wed ($200), Thurs ($200), Fri ($200).*

"For simple math, let's say that the average person earns $52,000 a year, which breaks down to $1,000 a week," George said as he pointed to the heading of his chart. "And if you work five days a week, it breaks down to $200 a day. When we consider the typical expenses involved, we can see that most people work every Monday, and part of Tuesday, just to pay Uncle Sam. This will vary based on your tax bracket. Then most people spend 35 to 45% of their income on their housing expenses. That can be rent, mortgage, utilities, taxes, insurance, etcetera. So, going back to our weekly breakdown, that is at least every Tuesday and Wednesday that goes towards your housing expense," George said as he wrote *Housing Expenses* under *Tuesday* and *Wednesday*. He continued updating his chart, writing *Food and entertainment, transportation, health care* under Thursday and *phone, internet, subscriptions, debt payments, misc.,* under Friday.

Dan watched as he wrote in each category and tried to quickly do the math, adding up his expenses in each of these categories. They were not exact, but they did come pretty close to George's assumptions. Tuesday and Wednesday would be $400 a week, times 52 weeks in a year which came out to $20,800 for housing which broke down to $1,733 a month.

"I know that everyone will be slightly different, but I have helped analyze the expense columns for hundreds of clients, and this is a very accurate income breakdown for a typical person that I work with," George said. He then wrote at the bottom in bold letters, *Which of these days can you control or stop paying altogether? Which of these days can you win back?*

Weekly Income Breakdown: $1,000 a week

Mon ($200)	Tues ($200)	Wed ($200)	Thurs ($200)	Fri ($200)
Uncle Sam	Housing Expenses	Housing Expenses	Food, entertainment, transportation, health care	phone, internet, subscriptions, debt payments, misc.

New Leaf Digital Whiteboard

THE IMPOSSIBLE HOMEWORK

Dan folded his arms and started to run a few hypothetical scenarios in his head. "Thursdays go to pay for food and entertainment. I guess you could reduce that by living off of ramen noodles," he said as a joke, but it stung because ramen had become his main meal over the last few weeks, and he was already sick of it. *There is no way I would be able to do that for an entire year*, he thought. He looked at Monday all going to Uncle Sam in taxes. He knew that last year he paid more than 20 percent in taxes, so there was no way he would be able to reduce that amount. *Housing?* Dan thought. *I cut my housing expense by more than half when I moved into Julie's rental, but I am still struggling to make it work. I don't see being able to reduce my housing cost much beyond what I am paying now*, he thought. "I can see shaving off a little here and there, but I don't think there is a way to win back..." Dan said with air quotes, "any of these days."

George nodded his head as if to agree with Dan's assessment. "This is the dilemma that most hard-working people face week in and week out. That is why it feels like an endless rat race. That is why most people think of real estate investing as something that they would never be able to do. They think it's for people who make more money when in reality, most investors do not make any more money than those who do not invest. They have just figured out a way to hack their lives and budget. Although there are so many ways to invest in real estate for retirement, in phase one of the plan that I help create for each member of our group, we always look to set up an aggressive plan that would help them achieve financial freedom in five years or less. Your sister Julie will likely hit financial freedom in four years," he said. He beamed with pride as he went down the list of people that Dan knew, who were already financially free, or had a clear target date of when they would be financially free.

"But to achieve such an extreme result, each of them needed to make extreme sacrifices. Every single person on this list has a dream. They dream of freedom of time and options do to what they want with their life. This is the result of financial freedom. Not everyone gets there," George said. "The number one killer of dreams and freedom is comfort. Every person on this list committed to make sacrifices and to be uncomfortable for a period of time intentionally. For most, that period is five years or less." George turned to Dan and asked, "If you knew that in five years you could be financially free and never have to worry about work or money again, what would you be willing to sacrifice in the short term to get that?"

Dan had already posed this question to himself while George was talking. All his stress, all his problems right now were financial. *I would literally give anything*, Dan thought. He turned to George and said, "I would do whatever it takes."

"Good," George said as he motioned back to the weekly income breakdown chart on the whiteboard. "How fast do you think you can start investing if you were able to set aside and dedicate the income earned from two entire days each week for nothing but real estate investing?"

Dan laughed. "Well, of course, if that were the case, anyone could invest. Two out of five days, that's forty percent of your income set aside for investing. Who can afford to do that?"

George smiled. "So, you agree? If you solved that one problem, you would have more than enough funds to start investing, correct?"

Dan felt like the conversation had taken a turn. He was frustrated because there was no logic to what George was suggesting. "We already went through this. Sure, we could shave off a few dollars here and there, but not enough to win back an entire day. And now we need to take back two days?"

"Exactly! Your assignment," said George looking at Dan to make sure he was paying attention, "before we decide whether the Cash-flow Breakfast Club would be a good fit for you, is to figure out at least three different ways you can take back your Tuesdays and Wednesdays."

Dan looked back at the board to see what those days were again, and his heart sank. "Tuesdays and Wednesdays are for housing expenses! So what am I supposed to do, live under a bridge?" He had just tasted the homeless life, and he definitely did not have any plans to go back to that.

George laughed. "Of course not. But there are many other ways to get rid of your housing expenses. There are many ways to live for free. Nearly everyone on this list has figured it out. Your assignment is to come up with three options for yourself and your current situation. If and when you do that, call me, and we can finish our discussion about the other requirements to be a Breakfast Club member."

Dan's mind was racing. *Everyone on that list had been able to get rid of their housing expenses? Julie was on that list. Was she living for free?*

CHAPTER 6:

Lunch with Julie

Dan stopped by the school where Julie taught and registered as a guest in the administration office. Based on the timing of the midday texts that Dan usually got from Julie, he knew her lunch was coming up soon, and he just needed to vent, or maybe ask her questions, or something, but it couldn't wait.

Let's grab lunch on your break. I'm already waiting for you in the office, Dan texted. He knew he was early, but he wanted her to see his message the minute she finished her class. They had met for lunch many times before, but this was the first time that Dan had stopped by her work to pick her up.

Woosh. A text came through. He jumped a little because he forgot that his phone wasn't on silent. The person at the front desk looked at him with a librarian-like raised eyebrow. Dan mouthed an apology as he switched his ringer to silent and checked the text message. *Cool. I'll meet you in the front in a few.*

Dan spotted Julie walking through the atrium, so he left the office and flagged her down.

"I'm starving," Julie said. "What are we eating?" Dan had put no actual thought into lunch as his only goal was to grill her on George's assignment.

"Let's do Zippy's," he said. "We can take my car."

The car ride was pretty quiet—the usual small talk. Dan didn't want to jump straight into a "George is nuts, right?" conversation. They pulled up to Zippy's restaurant and got a table right away. They placed their order when Julie broke the silence.

"Well?" Julie asked. "How did your meeting with George go?"

Dan took a sip of his Orange Bang drink so that he could take a second to choose his words carefully. "It was...it was frustrating. I went in to ask how much his program cost, and I left with an impossible homework assignment," he said, looking at Julie, hoping for a sympathetic nod. Instead, she gave him her infamous blank stare that said nothing but everything at the same time. "Come on, Julie. Help me out here. I can't figure out this guy. Every time I talk with him, I leave with more questions. Financially free in five years sounds too good to be true. Don't get me wrong, I want it, but I don't see how I can do that. Why can't he just lay out the entire program? The steps? The costs? I just need to know what to do, and I will do it."

"I would not be doing you a favor by giving you the answers ahead of time," Julie said sympathetically. "I understand your frustration. I felt the same frustration when I started the program. But I can tell you that if you can't do step one, then all the other steps will seem impossible. Step one gives step two a chance, which leads to step three. If George had given me all the steps upfront, I would have probably called him crazy, and I would have never joined the program. But look at me now!" she said, lowering her voice but keeping her excitement up. "A middle school teacher, a few months away from being financially free. You know how little I make, right?"

Dan knew because she was very open about her job and income. He remembered trying to talk Julie out of becoming a teacher because he knew how little they were paid and that it would be nearly impossible for her to support herself on a teacher's salary in Hawaii. However, she ignored Dan and much of the family's warnings because she felt like teaching was her calling. It was her passion, and she was great at it. She was often being recognized as an outstanding educator. Still, Dan knew those awards did not come with a financial bonus.

EVERYONE NEEDS TWO PROFESSIONS

As if reading Dan's thoughts and picking up where his train of thought ended, Julie grabbed his hand and squeezed. "George's program has changed my life. It allows me to do what I truly love doing, do what I feel is my calling, my passion, even though I don't get paid well for it. I remember crying a lot my first two years as a teacher. I was so fulfilled at school during the day but couldn't afford to pay my bills by the end of the month. I never told you this, but I actually applied for an administrative position at a real estate office because the starting pay was much more than I was making as a teacher. That's where I met George. He was the one that I interviewed with. Dan, I was a mess. I felt like I was a failure, giving up on my passion for a higher paycheck.

My internal conflict must have shown through because George told me that I could be great at this job only a few minutes into the interview, but I would likely be miserable. He said, 'You don't want to be an admin. Based on everything you've told me, you were born to be a teacher.' I broke down and started crying right in his office. My 30-minute interview turned into a two-and-a-half-hour therapy session with this person I'd just met. I could not believe what I was confessing to him, and how much about my personal life and personal finances I felt compelled to share with him. It was during this therapy session that George introduced the concept of passive income to me.

'Everyone needs two professions,' George said. That made me feel worried. I didn't feel like I had the energy for a second job. I poured everything I had into my teaching. But then he diagrammed out a chart on his whiteboard showing two professions. The first profession was for my money and my finances. He told me that if I put them to work correctly, suppose I put them to work where they have the single purpose of providing me financial freedom, then my second profession could be my passion regardless of the financial results of that path."

Tears started to well up in Julie's eyes. "Rather than give me a job, George changed my life that day. By the end of my therapy session with him, I had a five-year plan to financial freedom and homework for step one of that plan. I guess I had the same homework assignment that he gave you today. Get rid of your housing expenses." Julie looked at Dan and saw that her assumption was correct.

"Actually, I need to find three ways to get rid of my housing expenses," Dan said.

"Well, I can give you one-third of your answers," Julie said with a smile. "Option number one is getting your brother to pay your housing expenses for you."

Dan gave her a strange look as he tried to do the math. "You mean that my rent...?"

"Which is below market rent," Julie playfully interrupted.

Dan rolled his eyes and continued. "My rent is covering all of your housing expenses?"

Julie nodded. "To the penny. The renter I had before you was paying market rent, so I actually made $150 a month profit after paying the mortgage, taxes, insurance, and utilities, and setting aside reserves for capital expenditures and maintenance for the entire duplex, but you get the big brother discount. I have been living for free for the last three years. That is why I wanted this property. The numbers worked for my homework assignment. The financial pressure, the weight lifted off of me just by completing step one, was life-changing. It was only then that I could even begin to conceive of completing the next steps. I'll connect you with a few more people in our Breakfast Club. There are several other creative ways in which members of the group have gotten rid of their housing expenses."

Dan nodded in agreement, still somewhat shocked by what his sister has just shared with him. With that, they paid the check, and Dan drove Julie back to work. On the way back, Julie made a call to set up an appointment for Dan to meet with Sam the following day.

CHAPTER 7:

Lessons from Sarah

Dan watched as the waves gently rolled in and out, one after the other, as he waited for Sam at Duke's restaurant. Julie had connected him with Sam via text, and being that Sam worked at the Outrigger in Waikiki, he suggested that they meet right downstairs at Duke's. Earlier that day, Sam texted Dan to let him know about a last-minute issue at work and that he would be a few minutes late. Dan didn't mind, as this allowed him to enjoy the calm while he took in the sounds of the ocean. Growing up, he went to the beach every day. Now it was a rare occasion. The sun was overhead, but it was overcast and pleasant. Dan looked to the horizon; it was supposed to storm later that day, but there were no signs of rain clouds yet.

Dan started a list in his notepad. At the top, it read *Step One: Eliminate housing expenses,* and below that was a list of all the ideas he was able to come up with so far. *#1: Live under a bridge.* "Probably not what George is looking for," he said to himself, *but I didn't have any housing expenses for a few weeks.* Dan felt relieved to be in a place to laugh at his stint of homelessness. He continued down his list. *#2: The Julie Special - buy a multifamily property and rent out one side. #3: Buy a large house and rent out each room.* Dan heard about this one on a podcast that Julie made him listen to in the car the other day. *What was that podcast called? Something about big pockets?* He pulled out his phone and googled it. "Ah, Bigger Pockets," Dan said, making a note to subscribe to the podcast. He scrolled through pages and pages of results. He found their YouTube channel and saw a few videos on house hacking which seemed to be what Julie had done. *It looks like I've got more homework to do.* At the bottom of his notepad, he wrote, "Watch bigger pockets webinar on house hacking." He looked at his list and was happy that he got to three but felt like he needed to do more research to see if there was a better option.

That's why he was meeting with Sam today. Twenty minutes went by before Dan began to wonder if Sam had forgotten about their meeting. He checked his messages again. Nothing. Dan knew that Sam was squeezing him in at the last minute, so he wasn't too concerned. He started to draft Sam a text to tell him to meet up another day if he couldn't break away. "Dan?" He looked up to see a woman that he vaguely recognized.

"Hi, I'm Sarah. Sam is my dad," she said as she shook Dan's hand.

"That's right," Dan said, "I saw you at the meeting when your dad rang the gong."

She smiled. "That was a great Breakfast Club meeting. My dad apologizes, but the issues at work are still ongoing, so he is likely stuck there putting out the fire. I was supposed to meet him for lunch later today, but he just texted me to cancel. I told him that I was already here, and that's when he asked me to come touch base with you because he felt bad making you wait for so long."

"Oh, not a problem. It gave me a chance to take in the waves today. Plus, he was doing me a last-minute favor," Dan said.

"He told me that you needed help with your step one homework," Sarah said. "I would be happy to help with that if you want."

"You belong to The Breakfast Club, too?"

Sarah smiled. "Yes, I was initially there to support my dad because I was suspicious of some of the real estate investments that he suddenly wanted to make. You probably heard my dad's story of how he spent a ton of money on some real estate guru's course. Well, this sounded like the same thing, so I wanted to make sure he wasn't digging himself into a bigger hole. Then once I saw it work out for my dad, I asked if I could join, too."

Dan observed Sarah's face as she spoke. She was younger than him by at least a couple of years. Her mid-thirties, he guessed. Her long brown hair caught the sun from behind her as she took a seat across from Dan.

"How much did you cover with my dad?" she asked.

"Not much at all," Dan replied. "We actually only communicated via text. My sister Julie connected us, and he said he would fill me in on his story when we met today."

"Sounds good," Sarah said. "I'll fill you in on what my dad did for step one. And by the way, before we start, I have to say that I just love your sister! Julie is the one in the group that gave me the confidence I needed to commit to the program."

"Oh, you know Julie?" Dan said.

"Yeah, she's great. We are usually besties, sitting together at the club meetings, but you took my seat at the last meeting. Julie has told me quite a bit about you, so I feel like I know you already," she smiled.

"Don't believe anything she told you about me," Dan responded with a nervous laugh.

"All good things. Your sister cares about you a lot and has hoped you would eventually join our investor group. I have been telling her to invite you for a while now, but she said you were pretty stubborn." Sarah looked at Dan and scrunched her face a little as if to size him up. "And you would only follow through on the program if you joined on your own versus if it was something she wanted you to do."

Dan felt his face start to flush a little. *Julie wasn't wrong.* Throughout the years, there have been many things that she nudged him to do. Take this course, read that book. But Dan never followed through on any of it. "Well, I'm committed to getting this homework done," he said, trying to steer the conversation away from him and back to Sarah and her dad.

"Smooth transition," Sarah giggled. "Okay. George helped my dad take a unique approach to getting rid of his housing payment. Many in the group are trying to retire early and are younger. Many have families. Some are still at a point where they're looking to buy their first home, like me or like your sister was. But my dad was different. He was already at retirement age, and he and my mom had their forever home. They've been there a while, raised me there. They didn't really want to move to get rid of their housing payment. So first, they looked at a debt snowball to pay off their mortgage. If they took every penny of their disposable income and applied it to paying off their mortgage early, it would have taken them four years. That seemed like a long time to get step one done. Also, George explained to them that paying off the mortgage on their primary residence, while a huge step towards drastically reducing their housing expenses, wouldn't eliminate it altogether. They would still need about $1,500 a month for property taxes, insurance, and utilities. So, they decided to go the opposite route and leverage their equity to buy a cash-flow rental to offset their housing expenses."

"Wait, you can do that?" Dan interrupted.

"I was very suspicious at first as well. That's why I insisted that my dad run everything by me during the process. However, it turned out to be a brilliant option for them. So, at this point, they have lived in that house for sixteen years. They had an interest rate of 4.5%, but due to a combination of market appreciation and principal paydown through the mortgage payments over the years, they had about $275,000 in equity that they could pull out on an 80% loan-to-value refinance. However, even though they were adding $275,000 to their mortgage balance, because they could take their interest rate down to 2.75%, their new monthly payment was about the same as before. Technically I think it was like $43 more a month. But now, they had $275,000 that they were able to use to purchase an investment property that would bring in positive cashflow to cover their housing expenses. Over the next three months, my mom and dad broke that $275,000 into 25% down payments on three different small multifamily properties on the mainland."

"Why the mainland?" Dan asked.

"They were able to get more for their money and found properties that cash-flowed better," Sarah said. "The first few properties they bought were on the east coast near Washington DC. George owns property in that area as well, so he connected my dad with his broker and property manager there."

Dan was having a hard time wrapping his head around investing outside of Hawaii. He couldn't understand why George, who only got paid on properties he sold in Hawaii, would send his clients elsewhere. It did not make any sense.

Sarah pulled up what looked like a mobile version of a financial spreadsheet and pinch-zoomed on her phone to expand the bottom line. "Adding all three properties together, they bought just above the 1% rule," Sarah looked up at Dan to read his expression to make sure he knew what that meant. He nodded even though he had no clue what she was talking about.

Dan made a mental note: *Look up the 1% rule.*

OPEX/CAPEX

Julie continued. "So, after paying the PITI and OpEx/CapEx."

Dan interrupted by making a T sign with his hands, signaling a timeout. "I know PITI is Principal, Interest, Taxes, and Insurance, but what is OpEx/CapEx?"

Sarah laughed, "That's right, I forgot that you just joined the club. We use a lot of acronyms and abbreviations. OpEx/CapEx stands for

Operational Expenses and Capital Expenditures. This covers things like property management fees, vacancy rate, and repairs. It means we are setting a percent of the rent aside to pay someone else to manage it. We are also setting a percent of the rent aside in reserves to cover the bills when a unit is vacant, and some of it goes into reserves to pay for future maintenance and capital expenditures that come up down the road. So, after PITI and OpEx/CapEx, these properties bring in a PIFL, or Passive Income For Life," Sarah clarified. "Basically, a positive cash-flow of $4,833 a month. Mom and Dad's total housing expenses, including their new mortgage payment, taxes, insurance, and utilities, comes to $4,121. So in about three months, with no money out of their pocket, they were able to get rid of their housing payment completely and have an additional $721 a month of income which gave them a head start on steps number two and three. Overnight, my parents now had $58,000 of excess income each year to start their snowball real estate investing!"

Dan was scribbling down some of the numbers on a napkin. "I am having a hard time adding up the math," he said.

"Here, take a look at this spreadsheet," Sarah said as she got up from her seat and sat down on the other side of the table next to Dan.

Dan couldn't help but notice a hint of vanilla bean—one of his favorite scents--from Sarah as she leaned in to show him the numbers on her phone. She turned her phone sideways, and the spreadsheet rotated and expanded. As she scrolled back to the top, Dan saw that it read George's *Live for Free Calculator*, and under it were various color-coded boxes with a bunch of numbers.

"I know this looks like a lot, but it is quite simple," Sarah explained. "This top box is where we input the information about their existing home before they refinanced. This second box is where we entered the new interest rate and the amount of money they planned to pull out on the refinance. This last box shows the new total housing expense once they refinanced and the exact type of investment property they would need to buy. It also shows the return they would need to remove their housing expenses altogether. Like I said before, I was very skeptical about everything, but once I added up the numbers and saw the math behind the proposed solution, it started to make sense."

"To be honest, it makes so much sense. I'm surprised that more people don't do this. I think cash-out refinancing has a bad reputation.

Before the last crash, many people were refinancing to cash out the equity in their homes to buy liabilities that did not produce income, like boats or cars, or even spending the money on renovating their homes. All great in theory, but the moment that the market crashed and their home was no longer a piggy bank, most people realized that they were stuck with a new higher payment that they could not afford. After seeing both scenarios, I strongly feel that the only responsible reason to cash out equity in your home is if you are using it to buy cash-flow real estate that can more than cover the cost of the money that you cashed out," Sarah said.

Dan studied the spreadsheet on her phone and saw that the math was fairly straightforward. He put Sarah's phone down and shifted his chair a little. *Now that we are not hovering over a shared phone, we are sitting awkwardly close*, he thought. It was that feeling of being inside a crowded elevator, where it would be acceptable for someone to be inches away from you. But the moment the elevator emptied out except for you and the person right next to you, the mere inches separating you seemed way too close. So, naturally, you take a step to one side of the elevator to provide the needed space. *Do I get up and move?* Dan wondered. *That would be awkward as well.* Dan decided to pick Sarah's phone back up and zoom back into the spreadsheet as it was the only way he felt it made sense for them to be still sitting this close. "So, is this what you did, too, for your step one homework?" he asked, pointing to the third block on the spreadsheet.

George's Live For Free Calculator		
(Zero housing expense calculator)		
Cash out Refi - to Live for free calculator		
Current Home value	$802,500	
Current Mortgage Payoff amount	$350,950	
Annual Interest Rate of cash out refi	2.75%	
LTV% of cash out refi	80%	
Amortization Period (Years) of cash out refi	30	
New Mortage amount with Cash out refi	$642,000	
Estimated Refi closing costs (rolled into loan)	$16,050	
New Monthly P&I mortgage payment	$2,621	$4,121 (PITI)
Current Monthly P&I mortgage payment	$2,578	$4,078 (PITI)
Difference in monthly payment	$43	
Monthly Taxes, Insurance, HOA & Utilities	$1,500	
Cash Out portion only Loan Amount	$275,000	
Monthly Cost of Cashed out funds	$1,123	
ROI needed to cover cashed out funds	4.90%	
ROI needed to cover P&I mortgage	11.44%	
ROI needed to live for free (including utilities)	17.98%	

Cash-Flow BreakFast Club   Cash-flow Calculator   BRRRR Calculator   Rehab Est

"I wish," Sarah replied. "I didn't have that option. I had just bought my condo about a year before, and at that point, there was almost no equity in it because I only put 5% down when I bought it. I considered selling it, but after closing costs, I would have had to come out of pocket about $8,000 to get rid of it, and I did not want to do that. It was only a one-bedroom condo, so I couldn't bring on any roommates either to help pay the mortgage. I felt stuck. On the one hand, I was super excited for my dad. I saw how this one step completely changed his financial position and opened up the opportunity for him to start investing. On the other hand, I felt I missed my chance and would have to delay my financial freedom plan by a few years because I bought the wrong type of property. How could I have known that I should have been looking for a duplex or a large house that I could house hack or generate income from? They don't teach you this in school."

"I showed up to my appointment with George feeling defeated. I was ready to tell him that I would have to hold off for a few years, but George could sense my frustration. He had asked me how much my housing expenses were. I added everything up, and it came out to about $3,500 a month. George added it up for me and pointed out that it was $42,000 a year. He then asked what my housing expenses had been before buying that condo. I thought about it for a minute and replied, 'Nothing. I had no housing expenses because I was living with mom and dad.' He nodded. I remember a wave of dread washing over me. "I need to move back in with my parents, don't I?" He gave me one of his Zen responses. Something like, 'you don't have to do anything; however, anyone who has ever achieved something great, something exceptional' I remember him looking at me when he said that as if to let me know that my attempt for financial freedom at my age was exceptional, 'at some point had to figure out what they were willing to give up. And in most cases, it was their willingness to sacrifice their comfort for a period that gave them the ability to achieve something great.'

I remember so many worries rushing through my head. What would my friends think? How embarrassing would it be to let people know that I was moving back in with my parents? But when I moved out of my parent's basement to my condo, I gave up a lot of space for my independence. So, moving back in was really an upgrade to my living situation. However, the comfort I had to give up was my pride among my co-workers and friends. I would have to avoid trying to keep up with the Joneses, as George would say, for a few years so that I could carve out my own financial freedom path."

"But I thought you couldn't sell your home," Dan jumped in. "If you moved back in with your parents, wouldn't you lose money on the sale of your condo?"

SARAH'S SOLUTION

Sarah nodded. "After running a few different scenarios that day with George, I decided that I would rent my condo out and then move back in with my parents. I shot my parents a quick text to make sure they would be OK with it, and they said they would love to have me back. Eventually, I could rent out my condo, and after all the bills were paid, I ended up just about breaking even. I know that it's not a great start as a real estate investor so far, but because my parents weren't charging me rent, I now had an extra $3,500 a month, or $42,000 a year, that I would put aside for real estate investing."

"George warned me that most people who suddenly have more expendable income than before quickly find a way to expand their lifestyle and spending to use everything up unless they implement systems to stop them. I highly doubted that I would increase my dining-out budget by $42,000 a year. However, at this point, I was all in and asked George to tell me exactly what I needed to do. First, he advised me to set up a new checking account at my bank and label it financial freedom investment fund. Then he showed me how to automatically transfer $3,500 a month from my main account into this account every month. 'Although your tenant is now essentially paying your mortgage for you, pretend that you still have that mortgage payment obligation yourself,' he would tell me. 'Do not get tempted to use this money for anything other than your first cash-flow property.' The last key step was to remove this new account from daily view. He did not want me to see the money stacking up. He wanted it to feel like I was paying my mortgage and I was never going to see that money again. My bank had this option. I just had to check the 'hide' button for this new account. I could still access it and check on it whenever I wanted to. It just wasn't front and center when I logged in to my bank's app on my phone." Sarah paused to figure out if she should be sharing any of her next steps with Dan.

Dan saw her hesitation and jumped in. "Wow, what a sacrifice. I'm not sure If I would have been able to do the same. How long did you have to stay at your parent's house until you could move out again?"

Sarah laughed. "I am still at my parent's house. I am three years into my five-year plan. I took my $42,000 of redirected housing expenses that I was no longer paying and put that down on a duplex in the same area where my mom and dad have their cash-flow properties. It was nice not having to look for a new team as I was able to work with the same real estate agent and property manager that they were working with. We found the deal through their property manager, who told us that one of his other landlord clients was looking to offload a few properties, and this was the only one in my budget. I bought that duplex for just under $170,000 but was lucky enough to get the seller to cover most of my closing costs. The PIFL on that one is just over $9,000 a year. I followed the plan and snowballed that into my down payment for my cash-flow purchase in years two and three, buying bigger properties each year. I'm up to almost $35,000 a year of passive income and am only two jumps away from hitting my number. Once I do that, I'll buy my next place, this time putting a little more thought into a home that has potential for additional income."

Sarah realized she began to detail parts of steps two and three, though Dan had not officially moved on to those steps yet with George. "I hope that helped you with your homework," she said as she stood up, only now realizing how close they had been sitting this whole time.

Dan got up as well and thanked her for her time and help. He was still trying to piece it all together. It was difficult to wrap his head around all the sacrifices everyone in this group was making to stick to their financial freedom plan. Dan was not great at sticking to commitments and wondered if he had what it would take to do this.

> ### Sarah's Solution Breakdown
>
> Step 1: Get rid of housing expenses
> -Couldn't sell so rented her condo out to break even
> -Moved back in with parents for free
> -Continued to pay the $3500 a month that she was used to
> paying for housing, now towards her down payment account
>
> ---
>
> -She saved $42,000 ($3500 x 12) in her first year
> -She used that as a down payment to purchase a $170k duplex
> -That duplex has a PIFL of about $9,000 a year
> -She saved $42,000 again in year 2 + added the PIFL from
> year 1 to put down on a bigger property at the end of year 2.
> -She repeated these steps in year 3.

Sarah caught him by surprise when she leaned in for a hug, squeezed him, and kissed his cheek. "I am happy that you are thinking about joining the club. I know you can do it, and I'm rooting for you." With that, she turned and left.

CHAPTER 8:

The Price of Admission

Over the next few days, Dan found himself in his real estate office a lot as a past client reached out to him to discuss selling their home to trade up to a bigger house. It was great to have new business to work towards. He needed to close a deal or two to dig himself out of the financial hole he was in. As he threw himself into preparations for his new client, he couldn't help but feel a sense of worry and uncertainty. He felt as if he were a new agent again. He had no idea where his next client was coming from. He could no longer afford Zillow leads at their new price.

Dan stared at his office wall, searching for an answer. He noticed the homework list that he had pinned above his desk. He had not spoken to George since completing his list as he didn't quite feel ready for the commitment that it would take to make it. He read through the list again.

Step 1: Eliminate Housing Expenses
1. Live under a bridge (The Dan special)
2. Move back in with parents (The Sarah special)
3. House hack a duplex with a tenant (The Julie special)
4. House hack with a big single-family home and roommates (The Bigger Pockets special)
5. Cash-out refi and purchase cash-flow property (The Sam special)

Dan was sure there were more options, which was a change in mindset from just a week ago when he thought George was crazy for even suggesting it was possible. He underlined option number four. "I can do that," he said out loud.

There was something energizing about committing to his first step. He snapped a picture of his list and texted it George, alongside: *Can I get on your calendar to discuss the rest of the program?* He put his phone down and got back to work preparing for his listing appointment. He began to feel a newfound sense of excitement and connections that he hadn't seen before. A new client or a closed sale used to mean a commission check, and that was about it. But now, he could see the direct correlation between his next closed sale and his ability to take his first step towards financial freedom to buy his first house hack.

Dan received a reply from George with positive feedback on his list and a few suggestions for meeting times. He replied and confirmed a meeting for the following day.

When Dan arrived at George's office building, George was already waiting for him in the conference room just off the lobby and waved him in. "Great job on your homework. I saw that you underlined number four. Is that your preferred option?"

Dan nodded.

"Good," George said. "We will spend time looking at the types of properties that would work best for this situation, but first, let's discuss the cost of the program and the next steps."

Dan completely forgot about the cost of joining the Breakfast Club. Now worry and doubt started creeping back into his thoughts. *What if I can't afford it? Could I put it on a credit card?*

George walked over to the flat screen on the conference room wall. He pushed a button, and it turned into a digital whiteboard. He pulled out a digital marker and started writing. *Cost and Commitment to join the Cash-flow Breakfast Club.* On the following line, he wrote out *5050+10k.* He pointed to the first five and said, "the first commitment is to read five books a year that I assign to you. The foundation of all success starts with our minds and our attitude. Our financial success expands to the limits of, but not beyond, our financial IQ. We won't have enough hours in the day for me to cover each of these topics with you one on one, so I will give you five books that will lay the foundation for everything that we will work on as part of your financial freedom plan. It will help us to expedite your training and focus on the details of your plan versus just the broader concepts."

Dan looked at two books on the conference table. One was *Total Money Makeover* by Dave Ramsey, and the other was *Rich Dad Poor Dad* by Robert Kiyosaki. Julie had gifted both books to Dan a few years ago but he never read them.

George saw Dan's attention on the books and said, "yes, these are the first two books you will be reading. I want you to read them simultaneously. These two, in many ways, are contrasting. One talks about the evils of debt and is a very effective way to become debt-free, and the other talks about the importance of leverage in real estate investing. Understanding both concepts is important because both are correct when used right," George explained as he pointed to the next number on his whiteboard. "This first zero means a commitment to zero housing expense. You have already started this process with your homework. This next five stands for a commitment to purchasing a minimum of five cash-flow investment properties in the next five years."

"Why five properties?" Dan asked. "Why not just one or two big ones?"

"Great question," George said, thoughtfully nodding his head. "Early on, I did not have a minimum purchase amount as I based it more on the total cash-flow coming in. So, if you got there in one or two properties, that was fine. However, I realized over the years that the worst thing you can do is buy only one or two investment properties. There are three main reasons why you want to set your sights on five or more cash-flow properties. Reason number one, your first property is always the hardest. You are just learning, and you are not in investment circles yet, so you will likely buy an average investment at best. That's okay because it is just your starter property, and you can snowball even average returns into a better property the following year. Reason number two, by hiring the right management team, your cash-flow properties can eventually become fairly passive investments, but getting each property set up and running the way you like does take work. Receiving average returns after going through that work to purchase and set up their first property, many people become overwhelmed with the process and underwhelmed with the results and stop. However, the magic usually happens on your second, third, or fourth cash-flow purchase. You become a better investor, and as a result, better investment options start to find their way to you. Reason number three is risk reduction. I know that it sounds counterintuitive to buy more properties to reduce risk, but having one tenant is risky, if you think about it. Your entire portfolio lives and dies with the financial ability of this one person to continue to pay rent every month. If they stop paying, or if they move out, 100% of your investment cash-flow stops, and now you are responsible for 100% of the expenses until your property manager finds a new tenant. However, once you have five, ten, fifteen tenants, it diversifies your risk because if one tenant moves out, you have income from all the other properties to support your portfolio until a new tenant is placed. Does that make sense?"

"It does," Dan replied. "My parents had a rental property when we were growing up, and it seemed like such a burden on them. It was their first home that they bought together, and when they moved to their current home, they decided to keep their old home as a rental rather than sell it. They managed it themselves, and I remember their stress and how concerned they were every time a tenant moved out. They always eventually found a new tenant, but the amount of stress it put everyone through completely outweighed any benefits, especially because they were basically only breaking even each month."

"Ah, the 'accidental investor,'" George said with a smile. "We will cover that in detail during one of our sessions. But, just know that your parents' story is a very common one and is one of the main reasons many people are afraid of becoming real estate investors."

Dan scribbled in his notepad: *Ask Julie about accidental investors.*

"This last zero means zero consumer debt. Once you' read *Rich Dad Poor Dad* and *Total Money Makeover*, you will better understand the difference between consumer debt and business debt as an investor. Although they look the same, they couldn't be more different," George said, looking back at Dan to make sure he was still taking notes. "We will cover this in more detail at your first orientation session."

THE $10,000 MOTIVATION

"Lastly, this 10k stands for a commitment to risk $10,000. Motivation is a funny thing," George said, his tone now slower. "Earlier on, I taught people the exact same things that we currently discuss in our Breakfast Club. However, I didn't have a $10,000 commitment. Everyone started extremely motivated, but at some point, life got in the way. One by one, about 90% of the hopeful investors that I worked with found one reason or another, often excellent and legitimate excuses, to not follow through on their financial freedom plan. Since I've implemented this motivation element, we now have a 100% success rate of people following through on their plan. The same obstacles and legitimate excuses still pop up for most people during the program, but they are now compelled to look at them for what they are. Legitimate excuses are still just excuses," George said.

"I still don't understand how charging $10,000 is motivation," Dan said.

"It is not a $10,000 charge. It is a commitment to risk $10,000. Most people are motivated by the potential for gain or reward; however, the fear of loss is often a far more powerful motivation. To supercharge this fear, we tie that loss and the consequence of not completing the program to also the potential pain of knowing your money would go to a cause or organization you do not support."

"What?" Dan blurted out. "That's crazy!"

George smiled. "Yes, but it has a 100% success rate so far. Think about it. The fear of losing $10,000 if you don't complete the program is probably enough to keep you motivated for your first year or two. But after that, most people would write off that $10,000 as a loss, or it would be less of a concern because they would have earned it back in positive cash-flow. So, the motivation of the fear of loss will diminish over time. But, what if, in addition to losing $10,000, your failure to follow through also directly triggered a $10,000 donation in your name to a group, a cause, a political candidate, or a party that you did not support, or better yet, outright opposed?"

"Why would anyone want to do that?" Dan asked, still perplexed.

"That's the point. No one would ever let that happen. At some stage, we are all okay letting ourselves down and giving up. It's way too easy to do because life gives us so many curveballs that it's nearly impossible to stay on one path and to keep motivated for a sustained period. This is just the best insurance premium available to ensure we maintain motivation and follow through. Your check would go on the wall in my office, and every time we'd meet you'd be able to look at it and let it fuel you to not give up. Once you complete your program and achieve the 5050 requirements, you will get your check back."

"So, you don't cash the check right away?" Dan asked.

"Correct. You would post-date it five years from today, and it's only sent to your designated organization, cause, or party to get cashed if and when you quit or don't complete your program in five years."

This put Dan at ease. He could write a check to get started, even though he didn't quite have the funds to back it up right now. "Can I write the check out to a charity I support?" he asked.

"Nope. If you did that, there is a 100% chance that you would give up because you would eventually justify in your mind that you are okay donating that money to that charity. Giving to charity is great, but that is not what this check is for."

Dan stared at the board, re-reading everything as he thought it through again. These were unconventional commitments, but ultimately, he saw how it just might keep him focused and on track to doing this. He looked George in the eyes and said confidently, "I'm in! If you commit to teaching me how to do this, I am committed to everything you covered today."

"Welcome to the Cash-flow Breakfast Club," George said as he smiled and shook Dan's hand. He handed Dan the two books that were stacked on the conference table.

Dan excused himself and went to grab his checkbook from the car. As he was writing out the $10,000 check, he wondered to whom he would make it out. He asked George a few more clarifying questions and presented him with a few options he thought of. One idea was to make it out to the political party he did not support. Admittedly, Dan was not very passionate about politics. He has voted on both sides before, and when he did, he focused more on the candidate vs. the party they were with. Dan felt that writing a big check out to either party would likely sting. The other option was writing a check to his biggest rival, his nemesis throughout his real estate career, an agent named Erik.

"Erik with a 'K' and I run in overlapping circles, and he has been known to bad mouth me to my friends and clients to steal my business. I am all for healthy and fair competition," Dan said. "May the best man win. But Erik always makes it personal." Dan felt himself getting fired up just speaking to George about Erik. It killed him just thinking about handing over any money to Erik. He was hoping George would be okay with the first option of writing out a political check.

"Which of those options would bring you the most pain?" George asked.

Dan sighed. "Hands down, it would be the second option."

"Okay, then that's the one you choose. The bigger the pain, the more effective motivator it will be."

Dan took a deep breath and nodded in agreement. He wrote out the $10,000 check to Erik, post-dated it five years out, and handed it to George. Then he thanked George and left the office with books in hand. Chills came over him. He was overwhelmed with excitement, but at the same time he felt the gravity of the decision he had just made. It felt like his first day of school. He understood the tremendous work ahead of him, but the promise of new potential made the hairs on the back of his neck stand on end.

Cost and Commitment to join the Cash-flow Breakfast Club

5050 + 10k

5	Commitment to read 5 assigned books a year
0	Commitment to zero housing expense
5	Commitment to 5 Cash-flow properties in 5 yrs
0	Commitment to zero consumer debt
+	
10k	Commitment to risk $10,000

New Leaf Digital Whiteboard

CHAPTER 9:

The Debt Snowball

The next few weeks were a blur for Dan. After his commitment day, he realized that it would be so much easier if he joined George's brokerage. To succeed in his financial freedom plan, he would also need to get his real estate business back on track, and he knew it would make sense to leverage George for help with that as well. He was now working out of the same office as George and negotiated with Dwight to swap desks with him because he wanted to be across the hall from George. Once Dan made that initial commitment, and he knew that he was all in, no matter what, the right decisions became easier and easier for him. He wasn't a true reader, but he devoured his reading assignments and got through both books in about a week. Both blew his mind, and he would stop by George's office almost every day to discuss something related to a chapter he'd just read. Although *Rich Dad Poor Dad* and *Total Money Makeover* were nearly complete opposites in focus, George would consistently tie their messages together, harping on the importance of understanding the difference between consumer debt and business leverage. One took you down a path that would limit your financial growth and investment potential, and the other was crucial for financial growth and exponentially increasing your investment potential.

During one of Dan's regular pop-ins George revealed how he could achieve the fourth commitment, which was zero consumer debt. Dan would need to work to pay off all his credit card debt he racked up during his most recent real estate rut. George opened the Dave Ramsey book and jotted a few points on the whiteboard.

First, list all your debts, smallest to largest, regardless of interest rate, then make minimum payments on all of your debts except for the smallest one. Next, pay as much as possible towards the smallest debt each month until it is paid off.

Then snowball everything you were putting towards paying off the smallest debt into the next smallest debt.

George circled the word *snowball* and turned to Dan. "This is the genius behind this method. At first, it seems counter-intuitive as most would say, let me pay off the highest interest rate or the largest debt first, but Dave Ramsey knew that we would need to see regular progress to stay motivated. So, starting with the smallest debt leads to much quicker results and quicker wins. Also, it allows us to take the magic of this snowball concept and compound our efforts with every credit card that we pay off."

Dan felt like he had grasped the concept when he read the book but was glad that they were breaking it down because he had not gone through the exercise for his own debt yet.

George returned to the whiteboard and explained. "Here is a basic example. Let's say you have five consumer debt lines," and began writing on the board:

Line #1 is a $2,000 credit card balance where you pay a $100 a month minimum payment.

Line #2 is a $5,000 credit card balance where you pay a $200 a month minimum payment.

Line #3 is a $10,000 car loan with a $500 a month payment.

Line #4 is a $20,000 student loan with a $500 a month minimum payment.

Line #5 is a $30,000 credit card balance where you pay an $800 a month minimum payment.

"So, in this scenario, you have $67,000 in consumer debt and a total monthly minimum payment of $2,100. However, the way credit cards are set up, if you only pay the minimum amount, you are seldom paying down much, if any, of the principal, so it could take 10, 15, or even 20 years to pay off this debt. If you decided that you wanted to pay $1,000 a month more towards your debt distributed evenly across all your lines, it would barely make a dent in the time it would take to pay them all off. However, if you took the debt snowball approach and applied that extra $1,000 to line number one, it would pay that one off in two months. Now you have that $1,000 plus the $100 that you were paying as a minimum payment for line number one. You snowball that in with the minimum payment in line number two, and now you have a total payment of $1,300 a month. Four payments of that pay down line number two. Then you take that $1,300 a month payment and snowball it into the $500 minimum payment for line number three for a new total of $1,800 a month. Five months of that, and now you paid off your car! Then you snowball that $1,800 a month into the $500 a month you are paying towards line number four, and the new monthly amount is $2,300. Eight months later, you paid off your student loan. Then you snowball that $2,300 payment and combine it with the $800 a month payment for line number five for a new total of $3,100 a month. Nine months of that, and you are completely debt-free. You took what could have easily taken 20 years to do and shrunk it down to a little over two years. Genius!"

	A	Credit Card #1		Credit Card #2		Car Loan		Student Loan		Credit Card #3		Total	
		Payment	Balance	Payment	Balance	Payment	Balance	Payment	Balance	Payment	Balance	Payment	Balance
4	Min Payment	$100	$2,000	$200	$5,000	$500	$10,000	$500	$20,000	$800	$30,000	$2,100	$67,000
5	Extra payment	$1,000		$1,100		$1,300		$1,800		$2,300		$1,000	
6	Total New Pmt	$1,100		$1,300		$1,800		$2,300		$3,100		$3,100	
8	Month 1	$1,100	$900	$200	$5,000	$500	$9,700	$500	$19,700	$800	$29,500	$3,100	$64,800
9	Month 2	$900	$0	$400	$4,800	$500	$9,400	$500	$19,400	$800	$29,000	$3,100	$62,600
10	Month 3	Paid Off		$1,300	$3,600	$500	$9,100	$500	$19,100	$800	$28,500	$3,100	$60,300
11	Month 4			$1,300	$2,400	$500	$7,800	$500	$18,800	$800	$28,000	$3,100	$57,000
12	Month 5			$1,300	$1,200	$500	$7,500	$500	$18,500	$800	$27,500	$3,100	$54,700
13	Month 6			$1,300	$0	$500	$7,200	$500	$18,200	$800	$27,000	$3,100	$52,400
14	Month 7			Paid Off		$1,800	$5,600	$500	$17,900	$800	$26,500	$3,100	$50,000
15	Month 8					$1,800	$4,000	$500	$17,600	$800	$26,000	$3,100	$47,600
16	Month 9					$1,800	$2,400	$500	$17,300	$800	$25,500	$3,100	$45,200
17	Month 10					$1,800	$800	$500	$17,000	$800	$25,000	$3,100	$42,800
18	Month 11					$800	$0	$1,500	$15,700	$800	$24,500	$3,100	$40,200
19	Month 12					Paid Off		$2,300	$13,600	$800	$24,000	$3,100	$37,600
20	Month 13							$2,300	$11,500	$800	$23,500	$3,100	$35,000
21	Month 14							$2,300	$9,400	$800	$23,000	$3,100	$32,400
22	Month 15							$2,300	$7,300	$800	$22,500	$3,100	$29,800
23	Month 16							$2,300	$5,200	$800	$22,000	$3,100	$27,200
24	Month 17							$2,300	$3,100	$800	$21,500	$3,100	$24,600
25	Month 18							$2,300	$1,000	$800	$21,000	$3,100	$22,000
26	Month 19							$1,000	$0	$2,100	$19,200	$3,100	$19,200
27	Month 20							Paid Off		$3,100	$16,400	$3,100	$16,400
28	Month 21									$3,100	$13,600	$3,100	$13,600
29	Month 22									$3,100	$10,800	$3,100	$10,800
30	Month 23									$3,100	$8,000	$3,100	$8,000
31	Month 24									$3,100	$5,200	$3,100	$5,200
32	Month 25									$3,100	$2,400	$3,100	$2,400
33	Month 26									$2,400	$0	$2,400	$0
34	Generic Example: Payments factor in a portion going to principal and interest every month									Paid Off		Paid Off	

Debt Snowball Payoff

George put the marker down and turned to Dan. "Aside from the obvious benefit of being debt-free, what other benefits can you see as a result of this exercise?"

Dan went to the board, thought for a moment, and then circled the $2,100 monthly payment requirement. "With that monthly payment gone, your credit score will skyrocket, and your debt-to-income ratio will be much better, allowing you to qualify for better investment property financing."

George nodded and asked, "Anything else?"

After scanning the board for answers, Dan shrugged and handed the marker back to George.

George smiled and circled the $3,100 debt pay-off amount. "In this example, you are training yourself to make a $3,100 payment each month. So, once all that debt is paid off, you just continue to make that $3,100 monthly payment, but now into your investment property down-payment account. You won't feel a pinch because you are already used to making that payment. Except now you will be putting away $37,200 a year to save up for your investment property purchases."

Dan took out his iPhone calculator and quickly punched in the numbers to verify the math. He then added $8,000 of credit card debt to reflect his current debt situation. Next, he readjusted the numbers to figure out what it would take to get this debt paid off in exactly two years. Adding a $500 payment to the example accounted for Dan's extra credit card debt. It would take his total debt snowball payment amount to roughly $3,600 a month or $43,200 a year. Dan went to the board and wrote *$43,200*. He circled it and turned to George.

"So, if I can just get rid of my consumer debt and continue to put $3,600 a month away, I will have $43,200 a year to invest in real estate every year after that?" It was less of a question for George and more of a question to himself as he was wondering why he was noticing this for the first time.

"Yes. I know that you are also working on getting rid of your housing payment. How much would that free up for you each month?" George asked.

Dan pulled out his phone and opened the Evernote folder he had created to keep track of notes for this class. He quickly added up his rent, insurance, and utilities. "It comes out to about $4,150 a month, or $49,800 a year."

George added *$49,800* under the *$43,200*, and added them up. "So, once you get rid of your housing payments and all of your consumer debt, you will have a total of $93,000 a year freed up to invest," George said as he circled $93,000. "You could get a lot done with $93,000 a year."

Dan's head was spinning. At no point in his life, no matter how much money he was making, did he ever have $93,000 in the bank. *Could it really be as easy as following these two steps?*

George continued on the board. *Step #4: Debt Snowball to pay off all consumer debt.*

"You have just figured out step number four. Do you remember what step number one was?"

"Of course. Live under a bridge," Dan said with a laugh.

STEP #2: HIDE YOUR NEW CASH-FLOW FROM YOURSELF

George laughed. "Yes, exactly." And he turned back to write on the board, *Step #1: Get rid of your housing expenses.* He then moved to fill in the spaces he left between step number one and step number four and added *Step #2: Hide your new cash-flow from yourself.* He turned to Dan and said, "this may be the most important step. This is where you train yourself to ignore the Joneses. Since the creation of consumer debt and credit cards, most people have learned to live beyond their means. And as their means or income has grown, they've automatically expanded their lifestyle and expenses to match or exceed their new income. It is a cycle of poverty. It is the rat race. The more we expand our lifestyle and expenses, the more locked in we are to needing a larger income just to stay afloat."

George pulled up the stool next to the whiteboard and perched himself on it as he spoke. "I used to think that it was a discipline problem, and as long as you had self-control, you could overcome this rat race cycle. I eventually realized that even the most disciplined people would fall into the trap of trying to keep up with the Joneses. At some point, living below your means feels foolish. This is the same whether you have a $50,000 a year promotion at work or a new-found $50,000 of extra cash-flow because you found a way to get rid of your housing payments, or you found another $3,000 a month of cash-flow because you were able to get rid of all of your consumer debt payments. Discipline and self-control will eventually fail us all. Systems simplify our life and can automate what we need done. Most people use automation and monthly subscriptions to spend most of their income without even thinking about it. An unused gym membership here, a new streaming service there, and before you know it, you are spending more than you make, one twenty-dollar a month subscription at a time. However, if you used the same approach and automated the hiding of any new cash-flow from eliminating your housing expenses or debt payments, putting the money into a separate account that you couldn't view, track, or access easily would trick you into staying within your means just long enough to save up for another investment property."

George picked up his iPhone and held it up to illustrate a point. "We can run out entire lives from here," he said. "I love the convenience of technology. I do my banking from here. I buy things from here. However, the money that I am hiding from myself cannot be accessible from here. I purposely transfer those funds automatically to a bank account that I do not tie to any of my other online banking apps."

"That sounds like a hassle," Dan chimed in.

"Exactly!" George replied. "We all have moments of weakness. Moments when we are tempted to do something or buy something that doesn't align with our financial freedom goals. But if you must go through hoops to access those extra funds, it will usually deter most from spending it during a moment of weakness. This is an account you automatically add to every month, but you only access it to take out the funds once a year when you buy a new cash-flow property."

Dan thought about his old account at his previous bank. He switched to a new bank because of the better online banking options. Although he didn't use his old bank anymore, he still had just over $2,000 in that account primarily because that was the minimum to keep it open while avoiding the monthly $3 service charge. He always meant to take that money out, but it seemed like too much of a hassle to stop in and close the account. *Could this be my 'hide my new cash-flow from myself' account?* Dan wondered. It started to make sense in either case, and Dan acknowledged that he would work on getting step number two completed that week.

George returned to the whiteboard and continued writing. *Step #3.* "Sarah told me that she filled you in a little on step number three," George said.

Dan was taken aback. *Sarah was talking to George about me?*

As if reading his mind, George said, "Yes, we talk about you. You will learn at your Breakfast Club orientation meeting that an additional requirement that I have for each of the students is that once they reach the midway point of their financial freedom path, which for most is two to three purchases, they then start to teach and share what they have learned with as many people as possible. Then when we meet as a group, they get to quickly tell the group what principles they shared that week and with whom. This accomplishes two things. First, there is no better way to truly ingrain and lock in your understanding and learning than when you commit to teaching it to someone else. If you know you will eventually need to teach someone what you are learning, it triggers something in your brain, and you can retain more information and have a better understanding of the subject matter. It is a nice little brain hack that Jim Kwik talks about in his book *Limitless.*"

Dan sent himself a text as a reminder. *Buy Limitless by Jim Kwik.*

"The second reason I ask each of my students to teach and share what they had learned is that I truly believe that everyone needs to have access to this knowledge... this potential life-changing freedom. But it is not something that most people will be able to learn and act on by just watching videos and listening to podcasts. Those are excellent sources of knowledge; however, most people will never act on that knowledge unless they have a real-life mentor, coach, or advocate help them through the first few steps. I try to be that person for as many people as I can, but I am capped by the number of hours that I have in the day. But if each of my students commits to becoming a mentor and advocate to just one or two people in their lives each year, our reach and influence will radiate far beyond what we can get accomplished here in this office alone. So yes, your name has come up," George said with a smile. "You were actually the first person that Sarah shared her knowledge with, and she was excited to report this back to the group. She said she highlighted the basics of her snowball investing."

Dan did remember her mentioning that she snowballed the rent to buy her rental properties, but he did not put much thought into its mechanics.

Step #3: Snowball Investing for Cash-flow, George wrote. "We will spend a lot of time in our classes learning many different ways to do this. When you come to the Breakfast Club new member orientation meeting tomorrow night, and we will cover this step," George said.

Dan's heart sank. *Tomorrow night? How could I have forgotten?* He double-booked himself and scheduled a listing appointment with a potential client he had been working with off and on for over a year now. Dan had become used to making his real estate business his priority, and he usually dropped anything he was doing when he had a client meeting request as he knew those meetings usually led to new sales, and the more he sold, the more he made. He remembered booking the appointment a few days ago and, at the moment, despite knowing he would miss the Breakfast Club orientation meeting, he felt that George would understand and approve of him prioritizing business over anything else. He apologized to George and explained why he wouldn't make the meeting. He asked when the next make up session would be.

George's expression changed as he took in the news. "The next orientation class is in twelve weeks. We teach new members on a twelve-week cycle. I understand how important a new client listing appointment is for business. However, I don't think it is more important than taking your next steps to achieve your financial freedom."

Dan felt confused. *Does he want me to cancel my listing appointment?*

"Obtaining financial freedom in five years or less is not easy, and the only way you will make it happen is if you prioritize your future self above your current self. You need to sacrifice now to have a shot at an amazing feat of financial freedom in five years. Like most, you have an addiction to earning active income. It's understandable. Active income is important as it pays the bills right now. However, this addiction will be one of the biggest obstacles you face in your journey to create passive income. You have control over your schedule, and you get to choose when and how you work. The key is to make as much money as possible while still avoiding interruption to your financial freedom plan."

Dan had never met a real estate agent that didn't prioritize a potential listing above everything else. Did it make sense to risk losing this listing just so that he could attend the investor meetup? George seemed to think so. Still unsure how he would make it work, Dan agreed to be at the orientation as he had initially promised. Then he wrote himself a memo to try to reschedule the listing appointment to another day.

CHAPTER 10:

Orientation

The room was filled with nervous energy, much different from the main investor meet-up that Dan had attended previously. This time it was for new Breakfast Club hopefuls and inductees only. There were seven of them in the room. Dan sat at the back of the training area as he did last time. He could feel the angst exuding from the attendee seated in the row in front of him--a clean-cut guy who couldn't have been older than twenty. He was clearly over-dressed in a button-down shirt and tie. He looked around and saw Dan sitting behind him.

"Hi, I'm Kevin," he said, catching Dan off guard. They exchanged small talk, but Dan couldn't help but feel jealous of this kid. He was probably still in college but already focusing on his financial freedom plan. If he sticks to a five-year plan, he will be retired by 25. *What was I doing at 25?* Dan wondered. Just then, he saw Julie peek around the corner. She spotted Dan and waved.

"Why are you here?" Dan mouthed to her from across the room. She gave a wide-eyed smile and an expression that signaled that she was both excited and nervous. It was odd that she was attending this newbie orientation. It was even more peculiar that she didn't tell him she would be attending. Dan sent her a text earlier that day saying he was off to the Breakfast Club orientation. *Good luck!* she texted back. *Now she was here?*

George greeted Julie, and they spoke for a few minutes. Once George saw the clock hit seven precisely, he said something to Julie. She nodded and took a seat at the front. Then, he turned to the group and motioned for everyone to take a seat. "Welcome to day one of your path to financial freedom," he said with a smile. There were a few excited yells and cheers from the small crowd. "Although today is just orientation, everyone will leave here with the foundation for their individual plan for financial freedom. While you can speed up or slow down your financial freedom plan as much as you'd like, my request to you today is that you think big and dream big. Most of you did not know financial freedom would be an option for you until very recently, so why not push yourself even more to realize that you can achieve it faster than you could have even dreamed?"

MARATHON VS. 1 MILE

George turned to the digital whiteboard and wrote *Deciding to run a marathon,* then turned to the group and asked, "Who here has run in an official marathon before?" Kevin's hand shot up. *Of course, the boy wonder has run a marathon. Overachieve much?* Dan thought.

Dan remembered his first serious girlfriend was a runner and was often training for her next marathon. She tried to get him to participate a few times, but Dan had no interest in changing his diet, let alone all the running he would have to do leading up to it.

George called on Kevin and asked him to share the sorts of things one must do if they wanted to run in and finish a marathon by the end of the year. Kevin stood up like he was just called on in class by his favorite teacher. He turned sideways to be able to speak to the entire group. Besides Dan everyone was in front of him. This made Dan feel awkward as it drew attention to him in the back row.

"First thing I had to do was adjust my diet," Kevin said. I was not necessarily trying to lose weight, but my running coach told me what to eat, leading to more sustained energy. Then I had to map out an endurance plan. When I started preparing, I was nine months away. A full marathon is just over twenty-six miles. Up until that point, I had not run for more than a few miles at a time, and even that was a stretch for me. So, my goal for month one was to get to seven miles. My goal for month two was to work my way up to ten miles. In month three, I worked my way up to fifteen miles. In month four, I stalled and ended up digressing and maxing out at twelve miles. Realizing that I had hit a wall, I had to research how much time in the gym I needed to put in every week to strengthen my running muscles and endurance, and how much time to schedule for recovery after every run. I made a few adjustments, and in month five, I made it to twenty miles.

In month six, I hit twenty-six miles exactly, and in months seven and eight, I pushed myself to twenty-eight miles. I did that so it would feel easier when I did the actual marathon at twenty-six miles."

Kevin started to share details on fitness watches and apps, but George raised his hand and thanked him, signaling that was beyond what they needed to cover today.

"Knowing what you know now," George said, looking at Kevin, "is there any possible way that you would have been able to complete that marathon if you just showed up on the day of the event without any of the prep work and training that you did?"

"Definitely not," Kevin said. "I likely would have hit my wall and dropped out around the five-to-seven-mile mark."

George seemed pleased with Kevin's answer as he was working his way up to an analogy, and Kevin's input was helping. "Thank you, Kevin," George said and motioned to let him know that he could take a seat again. "Kevin seems like a fit guy, generally trying to live a healthy lifestyle," George said as he glanced back at Kevin and saw him nodding in agreement. "However, he still had to crank it up a notch and become a different person despite his fitness level. He had to start working out and training with focus and intent to work his way up to the ultimate goal of completing a marathon. His complete focus and determination to do difficult things that were probably not enjoyable to do at the moment, were all a direct result of him setting that big goal." George paused to let the parallel sink in between Kevin's marathon and financial freedom goals.

George turned to the group and continued, "Now, what if Kevin's goal was to get to one mile by the end of the year? Would Kevin have had to do anything differently?"

Everyone in the room shook their head no.

"Would Kevin have become a different person? Would he have forced himself to train harder and with the focus and intent that eventually led him to be able to run twenty-eight miles? The answer is no. Small and achievable goals," George said, raising both of his hands to make air quotes around the word 'achievable', "those goals do not push us to grow. They do not push us to expand. They do not push us to become a better version of ourselves. That is why I hate small and achievable goals. It's okay to map out small and achievable steps, but these need to be steps towards massive goals."

The atmosphere of the room changed. Positive energy replaced the nervous vibes from a few minutes earlier. The hairs on Dan's arm stood up a little. For the first time in his life, he understood the power of goals. Dan was never one for setting unachievable goals. He only set realistic ones, to which he saw a clear path. He never wanted to set himself up for failure, so he always made sure his goals were within reach. *How much more could I have achieved if I had just pushed my goals to be bigger and farther away?*

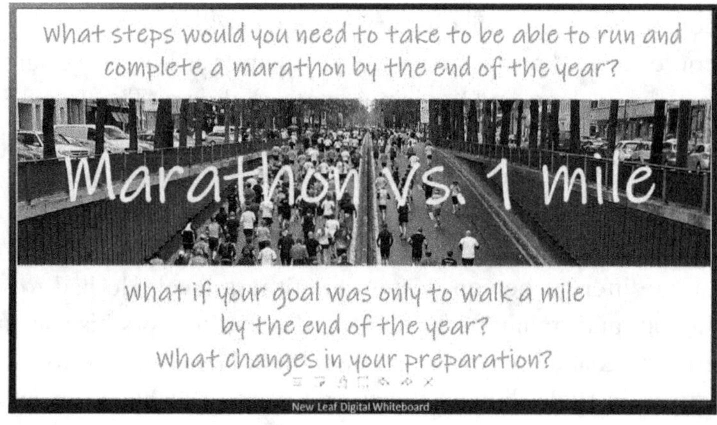

George wrote on the board *Marathon v. 1 mile*. He then circled *1 mile*, drew a line out to the side, wrote *One investment property,* and then turned back to the group. "Most of you here are looking to buy your first true cash-flow investment property, and that, in and of itself, is a great start. However, that is not and cannot be the goal. That would be like having a goal to walk a mile by the end of the year. Everyone here can do it. There is no preparation needed, and no one here will become a better version of themself because of this goal. Owning one cash-flow property will not change your life."

Dan had heard a version of this sermon before and knew what was coming. He smiled because he felt for the first time that he was slightly ahead of the game, or at least ahead of the class.

George continued, "The worst thing that anyone in this group can do is own a rental property." He paused to let that sink in. He saw Dan's smile and asked, "Dan, what's the second worst thing anyone in this class can do?"

Dan sat up a little straighter to respond, "That would be to own two rental properties."

"Exactly. This may sound absurd coming from a real estate investor, but it is true. If your goal is to own one or two rental properties, this is not the right group for you, and I am not the right mentor for you. Sure, I can help you buy one or two properties, but you will eventually hate me for it. Being a successful investor is a lot like learning to water ski. No one gets it on the first try. In fact, the first few times out on the lake, you will feel like you are drowning and may struggle to keep your head above water. You will contemplate quitting. You will exert a tremendous amount of effort trying and failing, until one day, you just get it. Something will click. You won't even know what it is, but suddenly you go from straining to keep your head above water to almost effortlessly gliding on top of the water. Owning one or even two properties is like trying to water ski but giving up before you make it to the top of the water. For your first few properties, everything is new. Everything often feels difficult. And to cap it off, the cash-flow from those one or two properties is usually not enough to be financially free or to significantly change your life. So, owning those one or two properties usually overwhelms you because of the learning curve and underwhelms you with lackluster results. And because of that, most people quit at one or two properties and swear off real estate investing as something that doesn't work for them."

George paused to look each attendee in the eyes. "Promise me that you will not stop until you are gliding on top of the water, having a blast. Know that you will struggle. That is a necessary part of growth. Most people get past that obstacle, and it starts to become easy somewhere between their third and fifth property. At some point, you will look back on yourself and wonder why you were struggling or why it felt hard for you. That is where your growth could skyrocket if you wanted to. Each of you have or will have a financial freedom road map that calls for you to buy one small cash-flow property a year. Buy your first in year one. Buy your second in year two. Buy your third in year three and so on. This is fine. However most in the classes before you found that their trajectory, rather than one, two, three, four, five was often closer to one, two, ten, fifteen, thirty. Meaning right now, you are still wondering how to get your first deal, but once you are an investor and get past the phase where you are trying to keep your head above water, everything becomes easier. Investment opportunities will start to find you and not the other way around."

George turned back to the board and circled *Marathon.* "Okay, so now that you know buying your first property is just walking one mile, what is your marathon? What is a goal so big that it pushes you to become a different version of yourself, a more focused and committed version of yourself?" George looked around and saw his attendees trying to do some version of extreme goal-setting math in their heads to come up with their new number.

THE BARE MINIMUM GOAL IS COMPLETE
FINANCIAL FREEDOM

"At the end of the day, it is not the number of properties you own; it is not the amount of cash-flow you have; it is what those properties and cash-flow translate to for you. What would they provide you? Absolute and complete financial freedom is the bare minimum goal that I allow if you want to remain in this group. Anything less than that does not make sense and is not worth the time and effort we will commit over the next five years. You can, however, set your sights much higher than financial freedom. Think about if money were no object, and if you were not tied to a job or daily commitment, what would you do with your life? Would you travel more? Would you spend months or even years abroad exploring the world with loved ones? Would you volunteer more? Would you make larger donations to your favorite charity? Would you set aside funds for your kids? Would you set aside funds for your grandkids? Would you buy investment properties for family members to help them get started down this path? Would you become a bank or Private Money Lender (PML) and make your extra cash-flow available to friends and family to use to partner with them on their financial freedom path? Would you finally take that risk and build the business you have been dreaming of building? Would you spend time focusing on your passion, whatever that may be?"

"Each of you has a financial freedom number that you need to get to. We assigned a PIFL amount and a property count to get you there.

Some are getting there in three years, and some are in five years. I want you to think of that number as your half marathon. For many, this will be a huge achievement by itself and will be a major milestone. Maybe one that you will be happy with as your final destination with regards to your real estate investment journey, and that is one hundred percent okay. However, also know that the real fun starts after financial freedom. Just imagine the moment you realize that your earnings from your job are no longer needed for you to survive. Your passive income now exceeds your expenses, and you no longer need to earn an active income. You can, at that point, choose to retire and do whatever you want with your life, not being constrained by needs of income and employment."

"Or you can choose to continue to work a little longer, knowing that one hundred percent of your income is now play money that you can use to do whatever you want with," George went on. "If you choose to continue to grow your investment portfolio, you can now look at different types of investments that may have higher risk profiles but also higher returns. At this point, you can turn the corner and go from financial freedom and security to creating generational wealth or leaving a legacy. Before moving on to our next step, I want everyone to write down their financial freedom number and label it your half marathon. Then determine what your full marathon goal would be." George watched everyone contemplate and come up with their numbers.

Next, he introduced Julie to the group as a guest presenter to cover the next segment. Everyone gave her a round of applause. Dan didn't know how he felt about this. He was proud of his baby sister, but it was also kind of awkward. Julie waved to the group, thanked George for the introduction, and seamlessly put on her instructor hat. Dan watched his sister as she confidently engaged the attendees with questions to gauge their understanding of the core steps to their financial freedom plans. Dan was impressed with her confidence and her command over the room.

"There is magic in this group!" Julie said. "You won't see it right away, but at some point, each of you will look back at what you were able to accomplish and understand that it was only possible because of that magic. Every person in this room will become instrumental to your growth and development as an investor and ultimately to your financial freedom."

Dan looked around the room, wondering if that could be true.

FIVE STEPS, FOUR PRIORITIES

Julie returned to the whiteboard and summarized the main steps and a few core principles.

- ◆ *Step 1: Get rid of your housing expenses*
- ◆ *Step 2: Hide your new cash-flow from yourself #IgnoreTheJoneses*
- ◆ *Step 3: Investment snowball for cash-flow*
- ◆ *Step 4: Debt pay-down snowball*
- ◆ *Step 5: Diversify investing once you hit your financial freedom number*

Priorities while on the financial freedom track
1. *Cash-flow*
2. *Leverage*
3. *Tax advantages*
4. *Capital Gains*

It was the first time that Dan saw the complete list. He hurried to take notes as his sister continued.

"Later today, George will go over a few investment snowball examples and really drill down on step number three. But before that, he wanted me to cover a few of the basics and a few important rules of thumb with you," Julie said. She pushed a button on the digital whiteboard, and a slide deck popped up with what appeared to be a P&L formula for a rental property.

"Let's start with the differences between someone that purchases a rental property for cash versus someone that purchases that same rental property with leverage," she said.

Line by line, she showed the stark differences in the Cash on Cash ROI (CoCROI). Her example showed that all things being equal, the same property would have a cash on cash return of 7.9% as a cash purchase, but it penciled out to be a 14.4% cash on cash return when purchased with a 25% down mortgage. She also explained the difference between CoCROI and IRR or Internal Rate of Return. She showed on the leveraged side, factoring debt paydown, tax savings through depreciation, and a hypothetical 5% appreciation of value in the first year, you would see a 43.3% IRR versus a 13.8% IRR if you purchased the same property as a cash purchase. Next, Julie started to detail some basic rules when analyzing cash-flow properties and how to calculate how much money to set aside for taxes, insurance, property management fees, vacancy rate, reserves, and capital expenditures.

Kevin raised his hand to ask a question. "What about equity and appreciation? How is that factored into these equations?"

"Great question. It doesn't factor in," she responded. "When setting up your financial freedom plan, you do not factor in appreciation."

This raised more than a few questions and objections from the group.

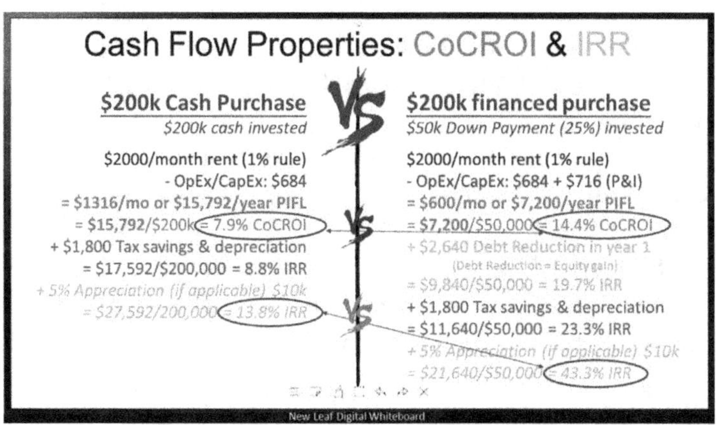

Julie turned to George to ask for a quick lifeline. He jumped right in to address the questions. "Julie is exactly right," George said. Appreciation and equity are game-changing aspects of investing in real estate. Fortunes are made with appreciation. However, it is also the least predictable aspect of real estate investing for a new investor. After you hit your financial freedom number, in step number five, you will likely look at more aggressive real estate investments that rely heavily on appreciation. Still, while you are building your financial freedom foundation, we will only focus on things that are consistent and predictable, and that is cash-flow."

Still confused, Kevin drilled down deeper on his question. "What if you need to sell your rental property a few years after you buy it, and there is no appreciation, causing you to lose money?"

George nodded. "Simple. While on this financial freedom path, do not buy a cash-flow property unless you are willing and able to keep it forever. If I buy a property for cash-flow today, and the value drops by 50% tomorrow, it would not affect my cash-flow plan because the cash-flow will stay the same. When I buy a cash-flow property, I never plan to sell that property. Have I sold before? Absolutely. Opportunities came up. I have been approached on multiple occasions by buyers making offers on my properties, and I sold and traded up to larger buildings. So, there is nothing wrong with selling your cash-flow properties, but you don't want to make a purchase decision with that in mind. If the deal is only good if it ends up appreciating, then it is too risky for you at this phase in your investing plan. Think of equity and appreciation as a bonus or a potential cherry on top of a great investment property. If it happens, perfect. If it doesn't, you still have a nice cash-flow property. Does that make sense?"

The nods around the room told George that it was OK to turn it back over to Julie.

RULES OF THUMB

Julie thanked him for his explanation and picked up where she left off. "Okay, now let's cover a few fundamental rules of thumb. First is the 1% rule."

Dan pulled out his pen again and started to take notes because he remembered this was on the list of things he was supposed to look up.

"Who can tell me what the 1% rule is?" Julie asked. One of the students explained that for a property to meet the 1% rule, it would need to rent for 1% of the purchase price each month. Julie gave her two excited thumbs up and thanked the student. "That is correct. So basically, if I buy a property for $100,000, I want to make sure that it rents for at least $1,000 a month. That doesn't necessarily mean it is guaranteed to be a good cash-flow investment, but if it meets the 1% rule, there is a much higher chance that the numbers will look good even after using a mortgage. The second rule of thumb is if you buy a small multifamily property like a duplex, triplex, or quadplex, then you want to shoot for a 1.25% rule. So, if you buy a $100,000 duplex, you want it to rent for at least $1,250 a month. The main reason is that there is often a slightly higher cost of ownership of a multifamily compared to owning a single-family home." Julie scanned the room to make sure everyone was keeping up, and she was pleased to see that they were.

PROPERTY MANAGER VS. SELF-MANAGING

"What about property management? Do you feel you can manage your own rental properties? Or should you hire a property manager?" Julie polled the room. Various students spoke up--some for and some against being their own property manager. Cost was the common theme for those who felt they should self-manage. Not wanting to have to fix toilets was something mentioned by Kevin, who was on the side that was for hiring a property manager. Julie gave everyone a chance to provide their input.

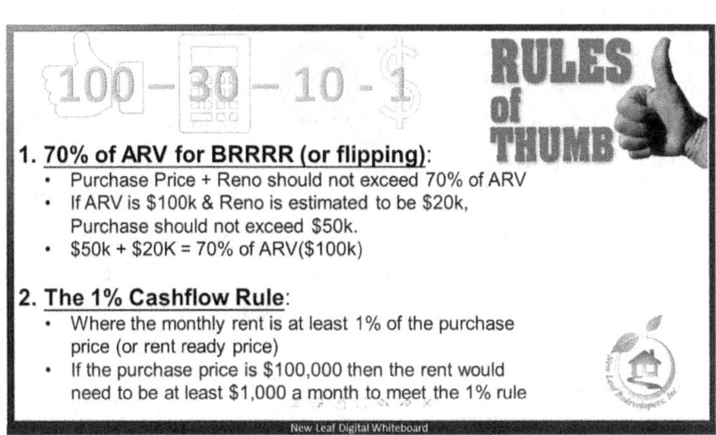

"All valid points," Julie said. "But ultimately, the most critical question to ask yourself is if you want another job or if you want an investment. Because if you decide to manage your own property, you are now trading your time for money or for saving money, and that means you have a job. It is not truly a passive investment for you until it makes money without your involvement. Now, most people can figure this out for one or two properties, but doing this at a scale of five, ten, fifteen or more properties is virtually impossible to do well if you do not have a good property manager or team in place. This is another reason most investors never make it beyond owning one or two properties. They self-manage, and the thought of adding additional properties means additional responsibilities, phone calls from tenants, and time commitments that they don't want to take on. Or maybe they would be okay taking it on, but their spouse or significant other starts to look at every property acquired as a new drain on energy and time away from the family. So to avoid this eventual drain and burnout, when we run our numbers to see if a property will cash-flow, we always factor in setting aside a 10% fee to pay a good property manager to run that property for us."

"I know that you are looking at that 10% as a reduction in your cash-flow, but I can tell you that, in reality, it is not. We buy from mom-and-pop landlords all the time who are self-managing, and in just about every scenario we have come across, they are under-collecting rent by at least 10% or more. If market rent is $1,000, they may only be charging $800 to $850. This is very common. So essentially, these mom-and-pop landlords have turned their investments into a very demanding full-time job, and they are not benefiting financially from managing it themselves. They pass on the savings to the tenants who usually know that they can get away with much more and get away with paying much less when there is no professional property manager in place."

Julie paused to see if there were any additional questions on the topic before she moved on. There were none.

THE HOA CONCEPT

She continued. "Who here lives in an HOA or condo development?" Many in the room raised their hand. Dan wasn't sure if he should raise his hand, but he did while shrugging to say he wasn't sure. He never bothered to see if Julie's duplex was part of an HOA when signing the lease. Julie smiled and nodded back at Dan to acknowledge that his guess was correct. Julie continued with a follow-up question.

"Okay, who here has ever served on an HOA or condo association board?" Most of the hands dropped. A lady in the front row kept her hand up. Dan recognized her from the front desk when he arrived that day. She had short black hair and a round face that was very kind and inviting. She stood out with a purple blouse that somehow seemed to be the color of her personality. Dan determined that she was either a new agent or an office admin that he had not formally met yet. He made a mental note to introduce himself to her tomorrow.

Julie smiled and asked, "Elna, would you mind sharing how your HOA board plans for and pays for maintenance, repairs, and major capital expenditure items?"

Elna nodded. "Those items are planned for, and the expenses are projected five, ten, and even twenty years out. Then they break down and spread out the cost of those items over the course of those years. Every month a portion of the HOA fee or condo fee goes into the reserves to build up until we need to spend that amount on that issue. For example, if we know that we need to spend about $100,000 to repave the parking lot in about ten years, and if there are a hundred homes in that association, then we take the $100,000 and divide that by a hundred, which comes out to $1,000 per home over the next ten years. So that would be an additional $100 per home per year or just over $8 a month that would need to be collected from each homeowner so that by the time we will need to spend the $100,000 to take care of the parking lot, we would already have the full cost saved up in reserves. We go down the list to do the same thing for all other items we expect to have to spend money on in the next five, ten and twenty years. Ultimately, that is how we determine how much the monthly HOA or condo fees will be. A well-run association will have consistent fees year after year without much fluctuation because they have thoughtfully planned for and capitalized their reserves for the upkeep of the neighborhood."

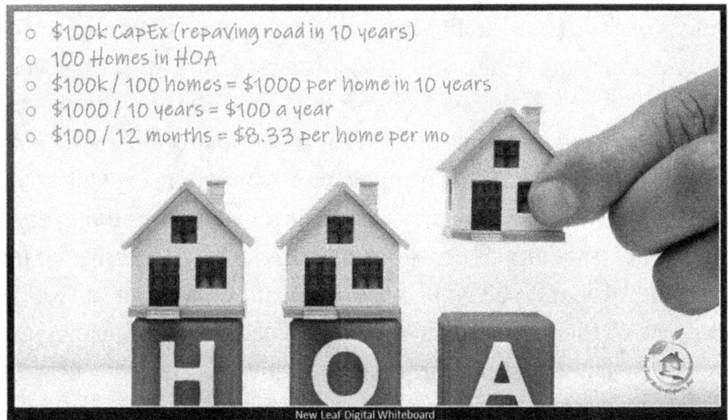

"Thank you, Elna," Julie said. "That was a perfect breakdown. Now let's take that concept and apply it to owning rental properties. You are your own HOA board. You need to make these repair and capital expenditure estimates and start to set aside reserves for those items on day one. For example, if your inspector tells you your roof likely only has five to eight years of useful life left, you get the roof replacement cost, divide it by five years, and start to set aside that amount from your collected rent each year. So clearly, just like condo fees vary from condo to condo, the amount of reserves you set aside will vary based on the property you buy. A very old property with a lot of deferred maintenance might require that you reserve ten to fifteen percent of your rent or more. But a brand-new property will likely need little put aside in the beginning. So as a basic rule of thumb and to help us compare all properties on an apples-to-apples basis, we calculate that we are setting aside a minimum of five percent of the collected rent each month for maintenance and reserves. Also, what you put aside when you own one rental is much different than what you will put aside if you own a hundred rentals. Your reserve per unit can drop the more units you have." Julie paused to allow everyone time to complete taking notes.

MITIGATING VACANCY RISK

"Next, we look at vacancy rate. Every area and region has an average vacancy rate which we look at when identifying areas to invest in. However, you can have a very undesirable property in a low vacancy area and still likely have a higher turnover than normal because your property is sub-par to the competition. Conversely, you can be in an area with a high vacancy rate of ten percent, but because you have a great property for the rate you are charging, you could have a very low turnover, thus, keeping your vacancy expense low. When you buy one property, you base your vacancy rate on how many months a year that one property is vacant, and you will set aside reserves accordingly to cover expenses while it is. For example, if you own one property, and your tenant moves out every year, and during the transition it turns out that it takes you exactly one month to place a new tenant, you will have one vacant month out of twelve potential months. One divided by twelve equals an 8.3% vacancy rate. If this were consistent every year, this would be your number to plan for. Ideally, you'll find good tenants who love renting your property and want to stay there for multiple years. If it turns out that you need to re-rent it once every twenty-four months, that would be a four percent vacancy rate. If you need to find a new tenant once every thirty-six months, that is a two and seven tenth percent vacancy rate," Julie explained.

"However, when you own multiple properties, you will start to group your entire portfolio together and track the vacancy rate of the portfolio and adjust your reserves accordingly. So, let's say you have ten properties, and you have one tenant move out each year, and your downtime is about one month. That seems like a hassle to worry about finding a new tenant every year. But in reality that is your property manager's job, and a good property manager often has tenants already lined up and interested in the property, so the downtime is minimal. And to calculate your vacancy rate, you would take twelve months per unit times ten units owned, which gives you hundred-twenty months of potential rent in your portfolio. One vacant month divided by hundred-twenty months equals a less than one percent vacancy rate. So, finding the right tenant is key, and having a good property manager that takes care of the property and the tenants so that they are happy is also important to the performance of your cash-flow return. As a rule of thumb, to compare different areas and properties as apples-to-apples, we always pencil in a minimum of 5% as our vacancy rate."

Mitigating VACANCY Risk

1 Door/Unit Owned: 1 unit vacant for 1 month per year = ?
• = 1/12 or 8% Vacancy rate
10 Doors/Units Owned: 1 unit vacant for 1 month per year = ?
• = 1/120 or 0.8% Vacancy rate
1 Door/Unit Owned: 1 unit vacant for 1 month every 2 years = ?
• = 1/24 or 4% Vacancy rate
10 Doors/Units Owned: 1 unit vacant for 1 month every 2 years = ?
• = 1/240 or 0.4% Vacancy rate
1 Door/Unit Owned: 1 unit vacant for 1 month every 3 years = ?
• = 1/36 or 2.7% Vacancy rate
10 Doors/Units Owned: 1 unit vacant for 1 month every 3 years = ?
• = 1/360 or 0.27% Vacancy rate

New Leaf Digital Whiteboard

THE ACCIDENTAL INVESTOR

"Okay, another thing that we'll cover today before we turn the time back over to George is the concept of the accidental investor." Julie tapped the digital whiteboard screen again, and it moved to the next slide, showing another line-item breakdown of a rental property. "We just spent the last few minutes discussing components of a good cash-flow investment property. Let's take the 1% rule to start. What is the average sales price in this area?"

"Just over $600,000," Dan answered. Julie smiled. She was pleased with Dan's participation.

"That is correct. Now, back to the 1% rule, do these properties rent for an average of $6,000 a month? Of course not. The average rent is probably about $3,000 a month. That is 50% of the bare minimum that we look for. So, at these prices, this neighborhood does not make a good cash-flow market. It doesn't mean they can't be good investments. They are just not good for traditional cash-flow investing. However, if you look around and start to analyze other neighborhoods outside of this area, you might find lower-priced properties that still have a good rental value. Now, look at the home that you are living in. If you moved out, would it meet the 1% rule?"

Everyone started to do some basic math in their head to determine where their home sat on that cash-flow spectrum.

Julie went around the room, collecting responses from everyone. "It looks like no one lives in a property that meets the 1% rule or even comes close. Does that mean you made bad purchase decisions? Of course not. You made decisions based on where you and your family wanted to live. I am willing to bet that not one of you factored in whether or not it would cash-flow well when you purchased it. And that's okay because you did not buy this home as an investment property. However, this becomes a potential issue when you move on to your next property and decide to keep your current home as a cash-flow property. At that point, you become an 'accidental investor,'" Julie said with air quotes. "You did not make a purchase decision on this property based on it being a good cash-flow property, so why are you now keeping it as one?" Julie pointed to the board and detailed an example.

Dan recognized this example as he remembered Julie having this conversation with their parents about their home when they were getting ready to downsize. *These are the exact numbers! I guess Julie has been teaching this class for a while now.* Dan started to write down the accidental investor breakdown from the board.

- ❖ *$400,000 Purchase price*
- ❖ *20% Down: $80,000*
- ❖ *80% Loan*
- ❖ *Move out and rent this property 5 years later*
- ❖ *$2,300 (Current market rent) - $2,089 (PITI) - $368 (OpEx/ CapEx) = -$157/month (negative) cash-flow*
- ❖ *-$1,884 Total (negative) annual cash-flow (-2.4% Cash on Cash ROI)*
- ❖ *$211/ month positive cash-flow (if not factoring in setting aside anything for OpEx/CapEx)*
- ❖ *$2,532 annual positive cash-flow (3% Cash on Cash ROI if not factoring in setting aside anything for OpEx/CapEx)*

Julie broke down the example exactly like she had broken it down to her parents a year before, explaining that the average accidental investor is cash-flow negative, or in the red, every month. And because of that, they decide that they cannot afford to pay a property manager. So, they give themselves the job of a property manager. Unfortunately, they also decide that they cannot afford to set aside money in reserves for vacancy or capital expenditures, so they end up paying out of pocket every time the property is vacant or something needs to be repaired. There were whispers in the group as a few of the students were comparing notes, realizing that they, too, were indeed losing money on what they thought was their first investment property.

CHAPTER 11:

Our Three Batteries

Julie returned to the whiteboard and pulled up a picture of three batteries. Next to it were several different types of light bulbs ranging from old school filament lights to CFL and LED lights. Then she labeled each battery: *time, capital,* and *DTI.* "When it comes to real estate investing, every single one of us has these three batteries. We all have a finite amount of time, a finite amount of capital, and a finite amount of DTI, or debt to income, which affects the amount of loans we are qualified for. In general, in the residential conventional loan market, each person is capped at having a maximum of ten loans in their name at any given time. So, if you own your own home, in theory, you should be able to get nine residential mortgages for investment properties. But, in reality, this DTI battery is often drained well before you reach ten loans. So, let's look at your cash-flow properties like they are light bulbs. The brighter they are, the more cash they bring in."

Julie reached into her school bag and pulled out a few props including various light bulbs still in their packaging and two flashlights. She turned to George, who was standing near the room's entrance. When she motioned towards the light switches, he turned off the lights. The digital whiteboard, still illuminated, provided visibility to the room, but it was much darker. Julie turned on what looked like a basic dollar store flashlight, and it glowed in the now dark room. "Older dim incandescent bulbs may still be cash-flow positive properties, but barely, and they drain the batteries quickly. On the other end, you have a very efficient LED light." Julie turned on her much smaller LED light, and it lit up the room like a torch. The beam was bright like a lightsaber Luke Skywalker would have used. Kevin made a Princess Leia comment, and the group laughed.

Now wielding her LED more intentionally like a lightsaber, Julie continued. "My lightsaber clearly represents much more cash-flow; however, because it is LED, it represents a much more efficient use of energy as well."

She directed her lightsaber beam towards George to illuminate the light switch and asked him to turn the room lights back on. She went to her props that she laid out, pulled up an incandescent light bulb pack, and held it up next to an LED light bulb pack. "This 100-watt light bulb uses 100 watts per hour. And let's say each battery can power this 100-watt bulb for one hour before the battery is drained. So, three batteries mean three lights would be your max capacity. Now let's compare that to the LED lights," Julie said as she held up the LED package.

"According to this package, this 100-watt equivalent LED light bulb only uses fifteen watts per hour. So that means my same three batteries can power six to seven times as many bulbs while using the same amount of energy, while at the same time being noticeably brighter. So, twenty light bulbs versus three light bulbs. Which is a better use of our battery power?" Julie asked the group. Everyone pointed to the LED lights. "Absolutely. So, most investors pull out a light bulb, plug it in, and are happy because they see the light. However, they don't stop to think about whether that particular bulb is the most efficient use of their battery power and how having that light bulb could impact, drain or even limit the number of bulbs they can power in the future."

"When investing on this financial freedom path, we all have three batteries to draw power from: our time, our capital, and our DTI. They all directly affect our ability to invest. To some extent, every property that we own draws on one, two, or even all three of these batteries. So that takes us back to our 'accidental investors' who buy a home, not as a cash-flow investment, but decide to keep it as a cash-flow investment once they move out. Sure, they have light. And that light is better than complete darkness. Some cash-flow is better than none. However, this inefficient cash-flow property is often one of the biggest obstacles that prevent them from maximizing their cash-flow potential based on their three batteries. All their free time may be tied up because they decide to self-manage, since paying a property manager means they would be in the red every month. Or they may have all their capital tied up in the property as equity, and they may end up using up most of their extra new capital as they spend money maintaining their property as issues come up. Most accidental investors do not set aside a percentage of the rent for vacancy or capital expenditures because they would be in the red each month if they did. Or they may not qualify for a mortgage when they find a better cash-flow property because their DTI is too high with their first property showing up as debt but not providing sufficient income to offset that debt."

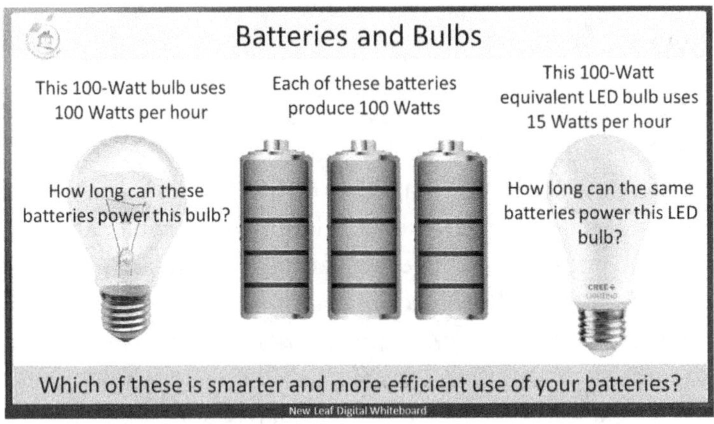

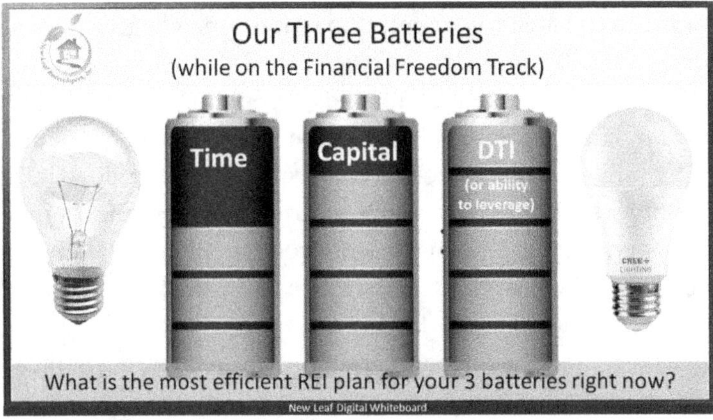

Dan looked around. The room was silent; everyone fixed their eyes on the board. Dan could feel the mental energy in the room as if he had just experienced a collective awakening. A universal a-ha moment that he was having, too.

Julie let the room stay silent for another thirty seconds, making eye contact with each participant, then she turned to George and held out her lightsaber. "Professor Yoda," she said with a smile. "Your JEDI trainees are ready for you to get to the good stuff and break down the investment snowball."

The room gave Julie a round of applause like they had just watched a play. Julie smiled and bowed. George announced a 10-minute break before they resumed the second half of the training. Dan walked toward Julie with a wide-eyed expression that she knew meant, "What the heck? Where did all this come from?" Julie smiled, and Dan gave his sister a big hug.

ARE YOU PLAYING THE RIGHT GAME?

"Wow!" Dan said. "Our class is lucky to have such an awesome guest presenter today." He recalled the conversations they'd had about Julie getting out of teaching because the money was terrible, and remembered Julie confessing that she almost did just that. *What a travesty that would have been. Teaching was clearly Julie's passion and calling. If she brought even a fraction of that passion into her classrooms, her students were the luckiest in the school.* Dan felt a chill down his spine as he was now seeing the full circle that the financial freedom path was creating for the first time. It wasn't about sacrificing and giving up passions or the calling for money or investing. Instead, it was about sacrificing temporarily to be able to commit to passions or callings, regardless of the money.

"How I wish," Dan paused to think through his next sentence. "I understand that I can be a stubborn ass at times. I also understand that I was likely not ready for any of this before now." Julie nodded in agreement. "But I wish like hell I would have come to you sooner, joined this group sooner, and started this process sooner."

Julie, still smiling, was silent because she could tell that Dan was still working through his revelation.

"My whole life, I have been focused on one game and whether I was winning or losing that game. I was obsessing with the game of earning money. Sometimes I would win and it was great! Sometimes I would lose and it sucked. I have been living and dying based on this scorecard. But today, I realized that I wasn't even playing the right game…I feel like I have been kicking a ball around in the mud all my life, not quite sure how to score. Sometimes I would kick it short, and sometimes I would kick it far, which felt good, but I never really knew the point of anything that I was doing. What happens if I stop kicking the ball? Is the game over? Who won? Who lost?"

He was talking to Julie, but he was staring past her as if he were watching himself kick this hypothetical ball around. "But then one day, someone comes up to me, picks up the ball, and explains for the first time that it is a basketball, and here is the basket, and this is how you shoot, and this is how you dribble, and by the way, this is offense, this is defense, and this is how you win. My mind is blown. I have been playing the wrong game my whole life. I feel like I just unplugged from the Matrix. Earning income is not what's important. Creating passive income is the only financial game that matters."

Julie smiled. "We have all been playing the wrong game. Just think of how much easier it will be for you moving forward now that you know which game to play. Now that you know the rules of the game and how to win. I'm still learning, too." She turned to look at George, who was conversing with another student at the back of the room. "We are lucky that we have a championship coach willing to guide and teach us everything we need to know to win at this game."

Julie saw George look at his watch and wrap up his conversation with the student. She hugged her brother. "It looks like we are starting again soon."

CHAPTER 12:

The Investment Snowball for Cash-flow

George cleared the digital whiteboard and wrote *Step 3: Investment snowball for cash-flow,* at the top. He turned to the class and waited as there were still a few conversations going on. Finally, Elna cleared her throat and said, "Ahem, Master Yoda is ready to begin." The class laughed and the last few people also headed back to their seats.

George smiled. "Thank you, Elna, for keeping us on schedule. I don't put money in the stock market anymore. Not to say you can't grow your wealth there, because you can. However, I find it to be a flawed system, and compared to real estate investing, much riskier. However, one aspect of the 401k and IRA concept is amazing. And that is when you allow compounding returns to work their magic on your portfolio. As an example, let's say you have a $100,000 portfolio. For the sake of simple math, let's say that it goes up by ten percent one year. You are usually not cashing out that ten percent to spend. Rather, you leave it in there and the next year you have a $110,000 portfolio to earn a return on. Once again, for simple math, let's say you get a perfect ten percent per year for the next twenty years. If you decide to take out those ten percent gains at the end of each year and only keep the original $100,000 invested, then at the end of twenty years, you would have a $200,000 return, which is $10,000 a year for twenty years. However, if you avoid taking out the returns every year and allow the law of compounding returns to take effect, that very same initial $100,000 investment would bring you a return of over $572,000. In this simplified example, compounding returns more than doubled the effectiveness of the investment."

George drew two lines on the board, one that showed a straight horizontal line angled up at a consistent 10% growth without compounding interest. The second line started on the same trajectory for the first three to four years, but right around that four to five-year mark, the line took a bend and started to curve upward at an exponential rate, showing the compounding effect. "It's beautiful," George said. He had a smile on his face as if he were discussing and admiring his favorite work of art.

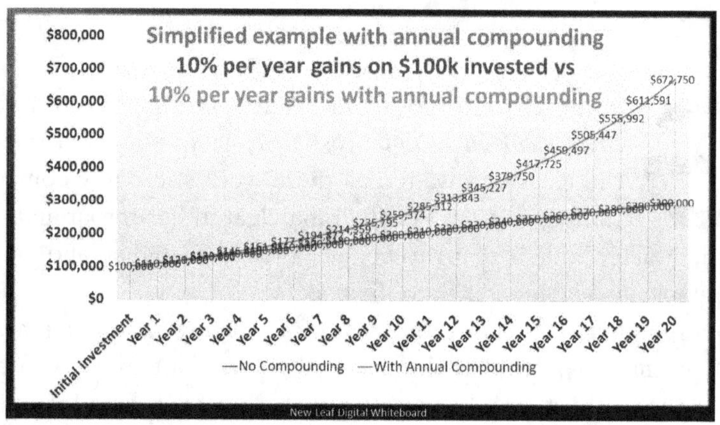

NOT APPLES TO APPLES

"Now, I believe that real estate investing is better than investing in stocks, bonds, Bitcoin, etc., in just about every way. They are not apples to apples. For example, you usually cannot take out a loan to invest in the stock market, whereas you can take out a loan to buy real estate. Let's say Kevin takes $100,000 and invests it in the stock market, and on the same day, Dan decides to invest $100,000 into an investment property. However, Dan uses that $100,000 as a 25% down payment on a $400,000 property. Let's say at the end of the year, the stock market and the real estate market both have great years and, for the sake of simplicity, go up in value by exactly ten percent. Kevin would have earned $10,000 and would now have $110,000 of value in his investment portfolio, but since Dan invested in real estate, that ten percent increase would be $40,000 because it was on the entire property value and not just the money that he invested. Now Dan would have $140,000 in equity, not to mention the $5,000 to $6,000 of equity he would gain in his first year as a function of debt paid down by his tenant. Based on appreciation and debt pay down alone, that would be a 45% ROI in the first year. That is separate from any cash-flow or any potential tax savings because of depreciation."

He then diagramed the same example, but this time, both markets went up by 5%, and once again, the real estate investment completely outperformed the stock market.

"Not apples to apples. I would say that it is closer to apples to mustard." George said. There were a few laughs throughout the room. "Sure, mustard is edible. Mustard can be delicious in the right quantities, but you would be insane to completely replace your apple intake with mustard. It just doesn't make sense. That being said, the ease for investors to take advantage of compounding returns within their retirement account is the one area that is far superior to real estate investing. Most landlords make a profit from a rental property, which immediately becomes income they can spend, and most often do. So, every year, most cash-flow investors invest with new capital but rarely take advantage of compounding returns. That is the reason that I created this program and this group. The investment snowball allows a cash-flow investor to roll over their returns every year and allow it to snowball or compound into a result much greater than regular investing."

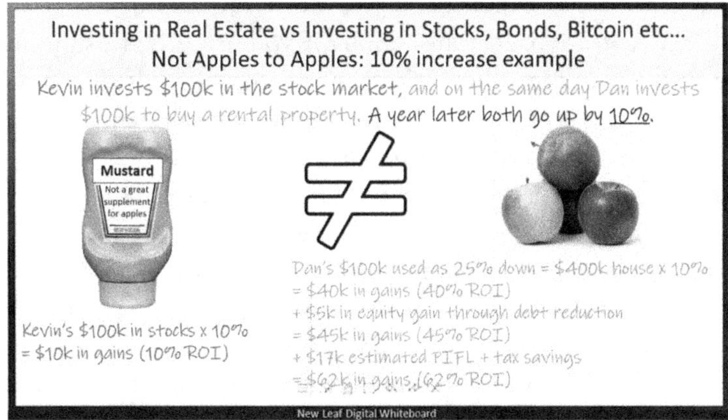

(What would the above numbers be for Dan if he used his $100k as a 10% Down payment?)

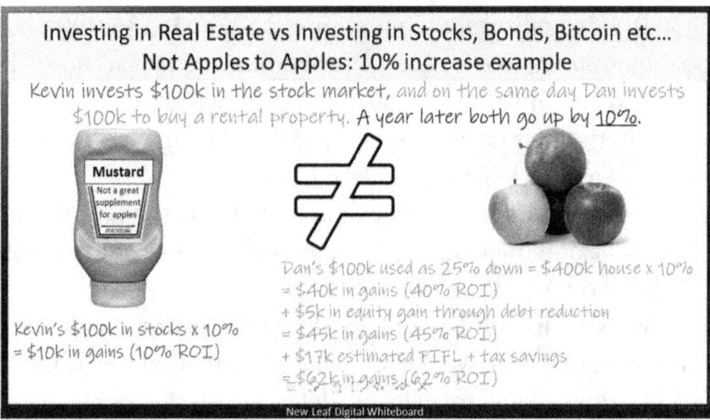

THE INVESTMENT SNOWBALL MATH

George tapped the screen, and the slide deck appeared. At the top, it read *10-Year $100k financial freedom path*. Below that was a financial breakdown of a rental property.

"I have already met with some of you to start this, and I will be meeting with the rest of you individually to calculate your exact financial freedom path through this investment snowball program. This generic example shows someone committing to invest $36,000 a year for the next ten years. This $36,000 would likely come from the funds they are setting aside once they accomplish step number one and get rid of their housing expenses. However, it can also come from savings, a few extra closed transactions if you are a real estate agent, a side hustle, or from your retirement account or self-directed IRA. It doesn't matter how you get it. It is just a focus and commitment to set that much aside every year to use as a down payment to buy one cash-flow property that meets our minimum standards Julie discussed earlier. After paying the property manager, mortgage, and expenses, and setting aside reserves, they would take that positive cash-flow, or PIFL, and add it to the $36,000 they are saving up the next year, allowing them to buy a slightly bigger property with a bigger return. In year one of this example, they buy a small property at $100,000. In year ten, they are still only bringing $36,000 to the table, but because they are rolling over the PIFL from their properties the year before, they can purchase a $450,000 property! This price range will allow this investor to evolve and grow over the years. Starting with a simple single-family rental, moving to small multifamily two-to-four-unit properties, and possibly even graduating to mid-sized multifamily commercial properties. In this example, at the end of ten years, this investor would own about $2.5 million in real estate. He would have invested $360,000 over that ten-year period, which is $36,000 times ten. However, during those ten years, he would have already received over $450,000 in returns or a 126% return on the money he invested. And the best part is if he stops investing at that point, he will have over $100,000 a year PIFL. That is $100,000 that he will receive every year for the rest of his life. That is an income that he can pass on to his kids and grandkids if he wants."

George's Financial Freedom Snowball-Investment Calculator for Cashflow

Year 10	Monthly Rent: $4,996	1.10 % rule			Per/unit
Realtor Retirement Program Calculator	VR + CapEx: 10.0%		Purchase Price	$454,164	$113,541
	PM Rate: 10.0%		Acquisition Cost	$9,873	$2,468
	Rental units: 4		Downpayment	$113,541	$28,385

P&L	Annual	Monthly	Unit/Mo		Per/unit
				Total Cash Invested	$123,414	$30,854
Rent	$59,950	$4,996	$1,249		
Additional Misc Income	$0	$0	$0	Out of pocket $ invested every year	$36,000
Total Gross Income	$59,950	$4,996	$1,249	Extra $ invested this year	$0
Property Insurance	($4,542)	($378)	($95)	Total annual cashflow on all units	$106,776
Property Taxes	($4,542)	($578)	($95)	Total number of doors owned	52
Property Management	($5,995)	($500)	($125)	Total $ of real estate owned	$2,504,568
Vacancy rate + CapX repair reserve	($5,995)	($500)	($125)	Combined Lifetime Total $ invested	$360,000
Total Expenses (prior to financing costs)	($21,073)	($1,756)	($439)	Combined Lifetime cashflow	$455,326
*Financed per terms below	($19,514)	($1,626)	($407)	Combined Lifetime CoC ROI	126.5%
Total Expenses, Financing and Reserves	($40,587)	($3,382)	($846)		

Net Cash Flow: PIFL	Annual	Monthly	Unit/Mo	CoC ROI	$ Down	Per/Unit
Passive Income For Life	$19,362	$1,614	$403	15.7%	$123,414	$30,854

*Financing Terms	
Amortization Period (Years)	30
Down payment	25%
Loan Amount	$340,623
Annual Interest Rate	4.00%
Mortgage Payment	$1,626.18

Year 1 Year 2 Year 3 Year 4 Year 5 Year 6 Year 7 Year 8 Year 9 **Year 10**

New Leaf Digital Whiteboard

"This income will not go down. It will, however, likely go up drastically at some point. What are a few ways that this PIFL might go up in the future even if you do not buy any more properties?"

Kevin raised his hand. "When rents go up?"

George nodded. "Yes, that is a good point. To simplify the calculation and remove the unknown out of the equation, when calculating your investment snowball plan, we do not factor in any rental price increases whatsoever, nor do we factor in any appreciation in value. However, historically speaking, most areas have seen a three to five percent increase in rental prices per year. So, assuming you could increase your rents by three to five percent per year, your $100,000 PIFL could increase by $10,000 to $15,000 a year. So, in year eleven, your $100,000 a year PIFL could be $110,000. In year twelve, it could be $120,000; in year thirteen, it could be $130,000, and so on."

George paused to let the note-takers catch up. "Let's say you are the most generous landlord in the history of landlords, and you decide that you will never raise rents, ever. If that were the case, what is another way your PIFL might go up drastically in the future?"

"What about when the mortgages are paid off?" Elna asked.

"Excellent," George said. "In this example, we bought our first property ten years ago. So, if you did not raise any rents, you will still have an increase in your PIFL when you pay off your mortgage in twenty years. Paying off that first mortgage would add about $5,000 a year to your PIFL. So, your $100,000 a year PIFL will go to $105,000 a year when you pay that first mortgage off. Then every year after that, for the next ten years, you will be paying off a new mortgage. At the end of paying off all those mortgages, your $100,000 a year PIFL will balloon to over $200,000 a year with no mortgage payments."

Next, George ran the group through a few more examples showing how to get to $100,000 a year PIFL in seven years by investing $40,000 a year, and how to get to $100,000 a year PIFL in five years by investing $65,000 a year. He then showed the class how on that $65,000 a year example, if you continued re-investing the PIFL for an additional five years for a total of ten years, you would have over $365,000 PIFL every year after that.

Dan was feverishly taking notes, trying to keep up. The first example was difficult to follow, but as George repeated the process with several others, Dan started to see the formulas' pattern and the simplicity.

How much money are you willing to invest every year? And what is your financial freedom number and end goal? If you gave George those two numbers, he would tell you exactly how long it would take you to get there. Or if you gave him your financial freedom number and told him your ideal time frame, George would reverse engineer the formula to tell you how much you needed to save and invest every year to get to your goal.

George started taking questions from the group. Kevin wanted to find out how soon he could get to $58,000, his financial freedom number. George quickly punched it into his calculator and gave him a few options. Elna asked about getting to $210,000 in eight years. George did the math and told her that it would require a commitment of investing $60,000 a year. Someone else asked what $100,000 a year for ten years would get them. George broke it down and showed that it would turn into nearly $600,000 a year PIFL.

Dan stopped taking notes and just watched George use math to answer question after question. Dan was never great at math. He could typically work out most problems, but this was something different. George was in a state of flow. It reminded him of the scene from the Netflix series *The Queen's Gambit*, where the main character (a master chess player) could visualize a chessboard in the air and see endless amounts of moves ahead of where she was. *We are all still trying to figure out our opening move, but George can see our tenth, eleventh, and twelfth moves before we've even started. George was Queen's Gambit-ing the heck out of this class*, Dan thought and smiled as he watched him wrap up the session.

Dan pulled up his notes from his last meeting with George. If he could get rid of his housing payment, he could save $49,800 at the end of his first year and would be able to buy his first investment property. He would simultaneously be working on his two-year debt payoff snowball plan. Starting in year three, he would have an additional $43,200 a year to invest for a total of $93,000. He waited for George to finish the class and went up to ask him to run the numbers where he invested $49,800 a year for the first two years, then $93,000 a year every year after that. Dan knew that he could survive on $105,000 a year, especially after paying off all his debt. However, he wanted a cushion, so he told George that his PIFL goal was $200,000. George put Dan's number into his calculator and showed him that he could get to $200,000 PIFL in seven years with that plan. Somehow knowing that Dan did not actually need $200,000 a year, George also showed him that he could get to $150,000 a year in year six and $108,000 a year in year five. George saved the results, printed out the five-year, six-year, and seven-year plans and gave them to Dan. He also wrote a note on the printouts and included a date that was one week out.

"What's that?" Dan asked.

"That is your homework deadline to lock in your plan. You have one week from today to review your plan. Decide if you want to work towards the five, six, or seven-year plan, and whether or not you want to make any changes. Once you are happy with your choice, we will lock it in and start taking your next steps."

Dan looked at the three plans. A week seemed like an eternity to wait for the next steps. He studied the different options: $108,000 in five years, $150,000 in six years, or $200,000 in seven years. He remembered what George said about just getting to the financial freedom number as step one, and once there, it would become much easier to get to bigger and better real estate investing. Although he really wanted to shoot for the $200,000 a year, Dan decided to focus on the five-year plan that would bring him $108,000 a year, and then worry about phase two after that. He signed the five-year plan and gave it back to George. "I don't need a week. Let's lock it in today."

George studied Dan's plan and seemed pleased with his choice.

CHAPTER 13:

The Walkthrough

Dan spent the next few days touring dozens of homes for sale. They were all large single-family homes with five bedrooms or more laid out in a way that he felt would be conducive to house hacking and renting out the extra rooms. Finally, Dan invited Julie to see his top choice. It was a five-bedroom, three-and-a-half-bath house in Makiki for $750,000. It needed a little work, but Dan was confident that he could take care of most of it himself. He was excited to get Julie's take. Ever since her guest appearance at his orientation, Dan saw Julie differently. Somehow baby sis grew up right before his eyes, and now she was a mentor that he turned to for advice.

Dan pulled up to the property and saw Julie's car waiting for him. He stepped out of the car and saw that Julie wasn't alone. *Who was that?* Dan wondered as he got out of his car and walked towards Julie's car. Julie opened her door to get out, and her passenger did as well. It was Sarah. *What am I wearing?* Dan thought as he looked himself over for the first time that day. *Board shorts and a t-shirt. Yikes!*

"Hey Sarah," Dan said. She waved back. Both Julie and Sarah had beaming smiles. "I'm sorry for my casual attire," Dan said. "This outfit is clearly hang-out with sister approved," he said with air quotes, "but not quite up to par for meeting with, ah, company."

"Don't worry about it," Sarah said, still smiling.

Julie raised her hand. "Ahem, excuse me. I think I should be offended here. So you don't want to dress up to hang out with me?"

Dan gave his sister a look and did his best to keep a cool expression while secretly pleading with his eyes, begging her not to embarrass him in front of Sarah. *This wasn't good*, Dan thought. He felt outnumbered, and there was a balance of power in their favor.

After some small talk, Dan made his way to the front door, opened the lockbox, and unlocked the front door. "Let's take a look," he said, motioning for them to enter. This put Dan more at ease. He had done this thousands of times and slowly slipped back in control of the conversation once he had his real estate agent hat back on.

CREATING VALUE

They walked through the main level and identified the areas where he could make a few modifications to the decor to brighten it up. An open kitchen, dining room, living room area, and family room were on the main level. Then there was a half bath, a large laundry room, and an office or den space.

Dan took out a measuring tape and measured the den. "Twelve feet by eleven feet," he read out loud. "This is big enough to convert into another bedroom if we added a closet."

Julie and Sarah sized up the room and agreed that the closet would fit perfectly on the back wall next to the window. Julie peeked around the corner from the den and saw that it backed into the powder room and laundry area. "Did you see how big that laundry room is? You could probably take half of that unused space and combine it with the powder room to make a main-level master bathroom."

Dan and Sarah both stepped out of the den to the hall to see into the den and the laundry room on the left at the same time.

"That's brilliant!" Sarah remarked. "With that one small change, you could convert this from a five-bedroom, three-and-a-half bath house into a six-bedroom, four-bath house fairly easily. My dad did something similar when we had to make room a few years ago to move grandma in with us. I helped get the contractor estimates, and I believe it cost about $10,000 to make the changes we needed. The plumbing was already there because of the powder room, so all they had to do was add the shower, frame out one side of the bathroom wall, and then add a closet in the office to make it a bedroom."

"Would you mind sharing your contractor's information?" Dan asked Sarah.

"Absolutely. Give me your cell number, and I'll text you his contact info now," Sarah said.

Dan shared his info, and Sarah replied with the contractor's info and three emojis, one smiley face, one star-eyed smiley face, and the emoji with three small floating hearts. Dan blushed. *What does that mean?* He caught Julie sneaking a side-eyed expression to Sarah that was communicating something, but Dan did not know what it meant. He couldn't help but feel they were up to something.

They moved forward with the rest of the house. There were three bedrooms and two bathrooms upstairs, two bedrooms, one bathroom, and a den downstairs. The lower level had a great feel. It had a separate entrance from the front, leading to a small private deck in the back. They concluded the tour and universally agreed that this was perfect for Dan. In converting the main level den and powder room into a master suite and making a few other cosmetic upgrades, Dan would spend about $15,000 out of pocket and put in some sweat equity over the first few weeks.

He then broke down the numbers. "Okay, the purchase price is $750,000. If I get a five percent down conventional loan, my estimated monthly costs of mortgage, taxes, insurance, and utilities will come out to about $4,300 a month. If I live in the main level master bedroom and rent out the five other rooms individually to students or office workers, I am confident that I can fill these up very quickly at $950 per room, per month. That comes to $4,750 a month total. So once this is fully occupied, the rent will fully cover all of my living expenses, and I will even have $400 to $500 extra each month."

"That's awesome. You can use that extra money to buy a bunch of air fresheners and hire a house cleaner every month. Just imagine six grown men rooming together. Think of how stinky it will get," Julie said, playfully scrunching up her face.

"Who said it would be six men? Maybe we invite in a few women as well?" Dan said with a smirk. Julie rolled her eyes, and Sarah laughed. Dan knew Julie was joking, but he couldn't help but think how awesome it would actually be to have his house pay for regular cleaners as well. *I wonder if I would be able to charge a premium rent if I advertise that it comes with regular professional maid service?*

They ended the tour outside, measuring out the driveway and parking area to ensure they could fit enough parking spaces for multiple tenants. They mapped it out and concluded that it would work. With Julie and Sarah's encouragement, Dan took the deal to George for his final stamp of approval, and he verified that it made sense to him as well. Dan decided to draft an offer. The market was hot, but this one needed some work. It had previously been a rental, and it showed. According to the listing agent, the landlord decided to test the market to sell because his long-term tenant had just moved out. He didn't want to spend any money on upgrades just in case it didn't sell right away because he only planned to re-rent it if that were the case. In fact, it was listed for sale and rent simultaneously. *Great.* Dan thought. *I'm not only competing against other buyers; I'm competing against renters for this house, as well.*

Dan wanted to negotiate the price because he was good at it; he often negotiated on behalf of clients, but this felt very different. He didn't want to lose this one. Sure, it would be nice if he got it for less, but the math checked out and worked even at the full asking price. After another gut check with George, Dan offered full price, but with a bit of back and forth with the seller. He asked the sellers to pay for his closing costs. That way out of pocket, Dan's down payment would be $37,500, and after closing, he would spend about $15,000 and some sweat equity to get the renovations up and running in the first two weeks. *All in for $52,500,* Dan wrote on his whiteboard at his desk while he worked through the math.

"Very doable. I'll be earning a commission on this sale that will give me about $17,000. I have a closing in two weeks with Mr. Jones, bringing in $32,500. My other transaction with the Yamaguchi family closes just a few days before my closing, and that will bring in $9,000. So, with these three closings, I will have enough for settlement." Dan looked at his math to double-check his work and was pleased with his results. "If you build it, they will come." At that moment, he realized that he was speaking aloud to himself. He scanned the room in both directions to make sure no one was eavesdropping on his conversation with himself. The coast was clear.

Dan smiled again. This time it was more than just about the math. It was more than just about this deal. It was about the progress that he had made in the last few weeks since committing to be financially free. For the first time in a long time, Dan was excited about both his short-term and long-term plans. He started with a big goal of financial freedom. With help from George, he broke the big goal down into smaller steps, and now that he was halfway through completing the first step, he felt like he was building the momentum that would carry him through every step. Everything was finally going as planned. He felt unstoppable.

CHAPTER 14:

The Fall Through

"What do you mean he no longer qualifies? Your pre-approval letter stated that Mr. Jones was approved to buy that house!" The office was silent as everyone could hear Dan having the dreaded conversation with his buyer's lender. "How much lower would the price need to be for him to qualify?"

As he hung up the phone, Dwight approached him. "Ouch. Any chance of saving the deal?"

"Not likely," Dan replied. "As you know, the market has shifted in the last two weeks, and interest rates spiked and rose by nearly 1%. Unfortunately, Mr. Jones was stretched to the limit of his loan qualification amount at the previous rate, but he did not have all his loan paperwork in and could not lock in his rate. Once the interest rate went up by a quarter point, I called him and told him that he should lock in his rate, but he was hesitant at the higher rate and wanted to wait a few days to see if it would come back down. It has not come back down, and it looks like it is stabilizing at nearly 1% higher. That 1% changes his payment significantly, putting him outside of the Fannie Mae qualification guidelines."

Dan felt like throwing up. Dwight did his best to offer encouragement, but Dan couldn't hear a word that he was saying because he had three different conversations in his head at once and had no extra capacity to take on another.

Dan went to the conference room to call his buyer. Mr. Jones picked up right away, and Dan went through the various scenarios and options. One option was to move forward with the contract and hope that the interest rates would come back down before closing. The problem was that tomorrow was the financing contingency deadline, and the seller was unwilling to extend. So, after tomorrow, if the loan did not go through, Mr. Jones would not be protected, and he would likely lose his earnest money deposit (EMD). His other option was to back out of the contract now to avoid losing his EMD.

"Which option should I choose?" Mr. Jones asked Dan. He was embarrassed by his mistake of not locking in his rate and was upset at the market and himself. Now he was willing to move forward with either option that Dan suggested.

Dan paused. He knew if this deal did not go through, it could jeopardize his purchase of the Makiki home because he was counting on this closing to have enough money for the down payment. However, he also knew option number one would be very risky for Mr. Jones and that he would have a high chance of losing his EMD.

"You should walk away from the deal," Dan said. "There is no telling when the rates will go back down, and it is just too risky to chance it."

After a silence that seemed like an eternity, Mr. Jones agreed. Dan hung up the phone, and they delivered notice to the seller. And just like that, Dan had his first fall through of the year.

He called Mr. Jones back to check in. Although he was bummed about having to back out of the deal, he thanked Dan for making sure he got his EMD back and told him he was ready to start looking for a new property that he would qualify for. Dan said goodbye, hung up the phone, buried his head in his hands, and sighed. He has had fall-throughs before. They were never easy to deal with, but it was part of the business. However, this was the first time a fall-through would get in the way of his financial freedom goals. Dan was three weeks away from closing on his Makiki home, and he no longer had enough money to purchase it. Dan knew he had to make the dreaded call to the listing agent to explain the situation and hope that they would grant him an extension.

He stopped by George's office to get his advice. After bringing him up to speed on his dilemma, George weighed in. "Now that you have a crystal-clear goal of where you want to go and what you want to accomplish, you will run into many obstacles on the path to getting there. There will be obstacles at every level. But, your job, and your only chance of reaching the finish line, is finding a way to push through and commit to making it happen no matter what, even if you don't know exactly how yet."

Dan would usually object and point out that it was out of his control, that there was nothing that he could do, but he had learned to take in George's Zen statements, to internalize them, and use them as motivation to find a solution.

George pulled out a calendar and counted the days until Dan's Makiki settlement. "22 days. You have 22 days until you have to close on this property. What do you need to happen before then to make sure it goes through?"

Dan did his best to push the emotions of losing his most recent transaction aside and started to do the math. "I need to find another client."

"Not good enough," George replied.

"If I found a new client today that put in an offer tomorrow and got ratified this weekend, we would need to close in twelve days to be able to keep our timeline," Dan explained.

"Which means?"

Dan looked at his timeline. There was no way a lender in this market could turn a loan around in that time frame. "Which means that I need to find a cash buyer who wants to close quickly."

George nodded. "Okay, go do that. Whatever your plans were today, cancel them, and instead spend the entire day going through your database to find that person."

Dan didn't even know where to start. After cycling through the gamut of emotions again, he decided to get the hard part out of the way. He called the listing agent for the Makiki property he was buying to explain the situation and ask for an extension. He knew the agent and they had had a good working relationship. This was the first time something had ever come up to jeopardize the transaction. After some back and forth with the seller, they figured out that they could spare three more days. It turned out that the seller was counting it close and did not have enough reserves to keep the property vacant for another month if the transaction did not close. Therefore, he would need to find a tenant right away to start paying rent. Dan hung up the phone after apologizing to the listing agent again.

Three more days didn't change much. He still needed to find a cash buyer right away. *How do you find a cash buyer that needs to buy now?* Dan was starting to feel his stress levels rise again. "Breathe," he said out loud to himself. After he calmed his nerves a bit, he uncapped a red dry erase marker and wrote in big, bold letters across his glass top desk. *I will find a cash buyer today! No matter what!*

POWER HOUR

Dan started scrolling through his CRM. He had thousands of names in the database. Many past clients and SOI, but most were names of people with whom he didn't have any real connection. Some were just old online leads that never panned out. He relocated to one of the back offices for privacy. He put up a *Do not disturb! Power Hour in progress* sign on the door and started dialing. He began with friends, family, and past clients, one after another, checking in to see how things were going. He wasn't coming right out and asking if any of them wanted to make a $1.5 million cash purchase, but he was probing to see if anyone needed to make a move.

Dan was a pacer. Whenever he got carried away on a phone conversation, he would usually get up and start pacing the room as he talked. Sometimes he would leave the building altogether and find himself at the other end of the parking lot when he hung up the phone. Each time he would look around and wonder how he got there. This call session was different. Dan propped a chair against the door, making it impossible to leave without conscious effort. He knew that every minute counted, and although he usually didn't mind his unconscious walks as he spoke on the phone, he knew that would eat into too much of his time today.

Dan made call after call, taking notes and updating his CRM. After three straight hours of calls, he was fried. He had spoken to over a hundred people. He had set up two listing appointments, one buyer appointment, and two networking lunches with potential referral sources, but no one came out and expressed a need to make a cash purchase this week. He was happy about filling his pipeline but still disappointed as none of these would solve his most pressing issue of needing a closing in two weeks.

It was 3:27 p.m. and he was starving. He removed the chair from the door and went to the breakroom to grab a bite and stretch his legs.

THE KEVIN BACON STRATEGY

Dan walked past George's office, but he didn't want to stop in without an update. He did, however, catch a glimpse of one of George's training manuals on his desk. It was labeled *The Kevin Bacon Strategy*. Dan remembered attending that training the first year he was in the business. George provided it for free to his entire office at the time. Dan always thought the name was hilarious. He was never quite a *Six Degrees of Kevin Bacon* fanatic, but he did play the game a few times. So, this training stuck out as it played off that theme where everything was related. One buyer, if handled correctly, would branch off into five or six new opportunities, and one seller, if marketed correctly, would branch off into five or six opportunities. Then, each of those opportunities would branch off into a few more, and so on. They were never more than six degrees away from achieving their business and financial goals. Dan went back to his desk and poured through his old, archived folders for any notes or handouts from that training.

"Found it!" Dan exclaimed. He opened the file and scrolled to the end of the handout because he remembered a very detailed list of activities that an agent could do to generate business, broken down into long-term branding and business growth, short-term lead generation, and immediate business generation. Dan had spent the last three hours mainly doing long-term relationship building and was able to pick up a few short-term prospects, but nothing that met his most crucial timeline. He needed another option to speed up the process. He found the page with the breakdown of short-term lead generation activities, including the one he was looking for. George called it "shaking the tree" or "looking for low-hanging fruit."

Rather than climbing a tree to search every branch for fruit, shake the tree first. The ripest fruit will fall to your feet. Using this concept allows you to take a large group of people in your database and filter them down to the select few that are ready to talk to you right now. This is easily done by sending a concise, straightforward mass communication to your group (or tree) that you want to shake. Finish with, 'Do you have a few minutes for a quick call to discuss sometime today?' Sending this message to hundred people will likely get twenty responses. Ten are 'No, or not right now' type responses. Seven are 'Maybe, or tell me more but later,' and three are Sure, I'm available now. Feel free to call.' This is your low-hanging fruit for the day.

Dan closed the book. "This is it," he said. "Hail Mary time."

FLOW

Dan grabbed his yellow hydro-flask from his desk and took a big gulp of water. He shook his hands out and stretched them a little to work out some of the fatigue and cramps he was feeling from his call session. He took a deep breath, and with a renewed focus, he locked himself back in the call room and began to scribble some notes. He was going to send a blast text to his database, but he had to come up with the proper wording that would bring cash buyers to the surface.

What would make a cash buyer want to talk to me right now? Who are cash buyers? he wrote on his pad in big, bold letters. Then he began making a list underneath that included investors and downsizing homeowners who had just sold their homes.

What would make a cash buyer need to buy now? Downsizing homeowners are rarely in a rush, so he struck through that option. Investors could move quickly, but they also rarely rushed into purchases. They wait for good deals.

What would force an investor to move quickly? Dan took a few more deep breaths. He could feel his breathing start to slow, and time seemed to slow down as well. It had been a while since he had been this intensely focused on anything. He could almost feel the synapses in his brain firing at a higher level as his creative juices were flowing. He flipped his paper over and converted his list into a mind map. Cash buyers led to investors in a time crunch which led to investors doing a 1031 exchange.

He circled *1031 exchange* and branched out from there. *I need to find someone mid-1031 exchange that is motivated to transfer their proceeds from an investment property sale into a similar investment property to take advantage of the tax-deferred status of the 1031 exchange.*

Dan was on a roll, in the zone, riding a state of flow, as George would call it. This term came from a book by Professor Mihaly Csikszentmihalyi. Dan never actually read the book, but George was borderline obsessive about the concept, attributing most, if not all, of his success to putting himself in short hyper-focused states of "flow," as described in this book. George would explain that many studies demonstrated that actual neurochemical reactions occur that allow us to operate and function at much higher levels while in these states of flow. Up until that moment, Dan always brushed it off, as the concept was a little too "new age" for him, but now it clicked. He could feel a change.

Dan drew a line from the 1031 exchange on his mind map and wrote *45-day timeline to identify a replacement property*. From there, he drew a line to another bubble where he wrote *Find investors who have sold within the last 44 days to see if they need to identify a replacement property or get under contract quickly*. Next he drew another line to the last blank space on his paper and wrote *The listing agent for the property that Mr. Jones just backed out of has not changed the status in the MLS yet to let people know it was going back on the market*. Dan had negotiated a great deal for Mr. Jones because he was willing to close quickly, which was important to that seller. That same negotiated price would be appealing to an investor, and it would likely be appealing to the seller, too, since a cash investor would be able to close quickly.

Dan scanned every corner of his now completed mind map to ensure all the dots were connected. They were. He pulled out another piece of paper and started to draft his text.

Hi {first-name}! You do not know me, and I apologize for the text out of the blue. My name is Dan Carter, and I'm a Realtor. It looks like you just sold an investment property that you have been renting, and I wanted to see if you planned to take advantage of a tax-deferred 1031 exchange. If so, I know of an excellent deal that is currently not available to the open market that my buyer just had to back out of due to increasing interest rates. If you are in a time crunch to identify a replacement property before your 45 days are up, this may be a great fit for you. Would this help your situation? If so, do you have a quick minute to discuss?"

Dan re-read his text to check for spelling and condensed it more. "Perfect!" he exclaimed.

He then logged on to several of his data subscription services and cross-referenced every closed sale in the state in the last 44 days that was non-owner occupied. This would imply that it was a rental investment property and would likely qualify for the 1031 exchange. He filtered to sales over $1.5 million because they would need enough proceeds to purchase the property that he would be suggesting. He then used skip-tracing software to pull up anyone not on the do not call list. Altogether he found seventy-three names that met this criteria where he could find a cell phone or email. He exported the list, entered it into his CRM, and titled it the *Hail Mary group*.

Dan was now moving at a pace that was beyond him. It was as if he knew the next ten moves ahead before he even made them. He copied his perfected text into his CRM's texting and emailing functions and queued up the message to all seventy-three contacts. One more deep breath in. Send. Exhale.

Dan watched as his *Hail Mary* message floated through cyberspace and returned with confirmed sends to fifty-eight people. Fifteen of the contacts had incorrect information, but this was expected. Dan continued to stare at his dashboard to see incoming responses to both his texts and emails.

Refresh. Nothing.

Refresh -one unsubscribe, then two, then three. Dan didn't flinch. This, too, was to be expected as he was sending this message out to strangers. Dan hated unsolicited messages from strangers. "I would unsubscribe too," Dan said to himself reassuringly. But he wasn't looking for someone like him. He was looking for someone who had been trying to do it all on their own to save a few dollars in commission. That person was likely just now realizing their mistake, potentially facing a six-figure tax hit. This person, whoever it was, needed Dan. This person would gladly have a conversation with a stranger if it meant it would help them save money and pull off a successful 1031 exchange.

Refresh. *Wrong number.*

Refresh. *Thanks, but I have an agent.*

Refresh. Nothing.

Refresh. Nothing.

Refresh. *Where's the property?"*

Exhale.

CHAPTER 15:

The Hail Mary

Dan got four positive replies to his *Hail Mary* text blast. The first inquiry came from a couple, Bill and his wife, Pauline. They had sold their rental property on their own to their tenant, so they did not have an agent. Just as Dan suspected, they could not find a suitable replacement property and were two days away from losing their ability to identify a replacement property for their 1031 exchange. After a quick call, they asked to meet with Dan that evening at the office.

After going over a few required disclosures and paperwork, Dan pulled out a 1031 Exchange worksheet. It was a simple form that George created to help identify how the capital gains were coming from the property they had sold and the price point of a replacement property or properties they would need to focus on to ensure they qualified for the maximum capital gains tax deferment. George was not a tax consultant, so he collaborated with a 1031 exchange qualified intermediary and CPA to create the form to verify the numbers. Pauline pulled out her stack of papers and notes that she took from the many conversations that she and Bill had had with their CPA. Dan used that information to fill in the blanks on the worksheet. Once done, he showed them the details of the replacement property that he had in mind. Because they only wanted to use the proceeds of the sale and not get a mortgage, the list price took it about $40,000 above what they could pay. Still, because Dan had negotiated a great deal previously for Mr. Jones, he was confident that he could get that same price again if they were willing to meet the seller's timeline. The numbers would line up almost perfectly, and Bill and Pauline were more than willing to close in two weeks if it increased their chances of getting it for a lower price--one that did not require them to bring any additional money to the table. Bill and Pauline gave Dan the green light to pull this deal together.

Dan called Mathew, the listing agent, to start working out the deal. "Hey Mat, I know that you must hate me right now, but I think I have a solution for you. I have a different buyer that is willing to step in to buy your client's property for the same price and can close on the same date that my previous buyer was scheduled to close on."

The phone was silent for a few seconds. "Is this a joke?"

"Far from it," Dan replied.

"I just got off the phone with my seller, and he was so angry about our deal falling apart. He blamed me for not staying on top of the buyers and not getting this wrapped up before the interest rates rose. He's contemplating pulling the listing from me and renting the unit out because he doesn't want to keep it vacant any longer."

"I am sorry for the trouble our deal falling apart has caused. But if you can show the seller our new offer, I know he will be happy with it."

"It's not that simple," Mathew replied. "The seller is mad, and I know that he doesn't want to talk to me right now."

After some back and forth, Dan proposed that he get the seller on a conference call so that Dan could apologize for the fall-through of the purchase contract and explain that it was in no way Mathew's fault. Then Dan would also explain the terms of the offer from his new buyers to try to get an agreement today. Mathew thought about it and agreed with the proposal. He got the seller on the phone to explain Dan's proposal, then called Dan back to make the conference call connection.

Dan spent the first few minutes addressing the frustrations of the seller and offered his apology for the previous contract not going through. He explained in detail what led to the situation. Ultimately the seller saw it was an unforeseen circumstance, and there really would have been no way for Mathew to prevent it. There was still a hint of frustration left in the seller's voice, but the tone of the conversation got friendlier. Dan felt this was the best time to detail his solution, which involved Bill and Pauline making a cash offer for the same price that Dan had previously negotiated for Mr. Jones. Since it was cash, they could close very quickly and stay on the original schedule. However, they could not go back and forth for days negotiating as is often common for this to work. It would only work if they could ratify that night due to their 1031 exchange timeline. After a few questions, the seller agreed to sell the property to Dan's new buyers at the same price if they could close in ten days. This would save the seller from having to make another mortgage payment.

Dan stepped back into the conference room where Bill and Pauline were waiting to relay the seller's request. They gave him an enthusiastic thumbs up. "We have a deal. I'll get the paperwork to you shortly, and we will make this official tonight," Dan said, concluding their call.

Bill and Pauline were ecstatic. Mathew was relieved. The seller was happy. Dan was still riding in his state of flow. So, everything went exactly as he expected: a true win-win for everyone involved. Dan sent the purchase agreement to everyone to review and sign, and it was ratified shortly after.

The following ten days flew by. Dan navigated the buyer's inspection without any surprises. He connected everyone with his go-to title attorney and settlement company. They researched the chain of title, also without any issues. Finally, the settlement company worked with the seller's bank to get their mortgage pay-off information for the new closing date--all clear.

It was settlement day at last. Dan, Mathew, the buyers, and the sellers were all waiting in the lobby at the settlement office. There were a few exchanges of pleasantries but mostly uncomfortable, awkward conversations about the weather and football. Everything except the real estate transaction that they were there to finalize. Dan decided to rip the band-aid off.

"As I mentioned before, thank you very much for working with us to speed up our negotiations when we spoke just over a week ago. We were in a time crunch, and your willingness to allow us to connect and streamline our conversations is really what made this deal possible. So, thank you," Dan said to Mathew and the seller. Bill and Pauline nodded their heads in agreement and voiced their appreciation as well.

The seller listened with an appreciative expression, searching for the right words. "Although this has been a great investment property for me," he said slowly, "I am not an investor. We used to live in the property you are buying today, and we loved it, but we had to move out over fifteen years ago, to get a place large enough to allow my parents to move in with us so that we could take care of them. The market wasn't great at the time, and we couldn't sell it. So, we were forced to rent it to help pay for the mortgage because we couldn't afford both mortgages." The seller stopped and wondered how much he should be sharing. He decided to continue. "We became investors by accident. We didn't know what we were doing. We made a lot of mistakes, but we learned a lot and got lucky too. We had some great tenants and a few that stressed us out. We loved this home, but ultimately, we are not cut out to be landlords. The small issues that popped up over the years and difficult tenants that we have dealt with have been a constant strain on my family for the last fifteen years." The seller finished his story just as the title attorney entered the conference room. "Thank you, is what I meant to say. If you hadn't come in when you did, I would have had to rent it out again, prolonging this stress for my family for a few more years."

Bill and Pauline smiled and thanked him. "It sounds like this was great for all parties," Pauline added.

The couple had a very reassuring presence about them. More than his regular clients, they reminded Dan of his grandparents. They were sweet and thoughtful.

Bill shared their vision of the property, which involved turning it over to their vacation rental property manager. They would lease it out furnished for 30-day stays, as they have done with several properties because they really enjoyed the creative aspect of the hospitality business. They were not just providing a place to stay; they tried to create experiences that their guests would remember forever. Dan had never dealt with vacation rentals before, and when Bill and Pauline explained their plans to him, he had to check the condo rules and the zoning information to make sure it would be allowed in this building. After they broke down the economics, it sounded like a great business. They were able to charge a premium compared to the average long-term rental rate, and compared to a month in a hotel, it was a great deal. They only needed to find twelve tenants a year, and their property manager usually had people lined up waiting year-round.

The settlement agent passed the closing statement around the table and explained form after form. Everyone read through and signed. Dan ushered the group together, and they took a celebratory photo to commemorate the closing. After the final handshakes and hugs, the group started to leave.

Mathew pulled Dan aside as they were walking back to their cars. "Do you have time to grab lunch next week?"

"Sure, I know a great spot," Dan replied.

"Excellent. I have always been impressed with your business, but I have recently seen a noticeable change in you. You seem inspired. I would love to know what's changed. Maybe, we can find a way to do more business together."

"I would like that," Dan said. They confirmed a time, then both got in their cars and drove off.

CHAPTER 16:

Bill & Pauline

The next day, Dan met Bill and Pauline at the property and was excited to help them with their preparations as he was intrigued to learn more about their business model. He spent most of the day helping Bill measure each room while Pauline followed along and sketched out designs and staging ideas on an art pad. Dan was impressed by her professional artist-level talent. She even brought pastels with her, which she used to add color to her sketches as inspiration hit. Every room became a work of art, a portrait, a masterpiece in her eyes. By the end of the day, they had everything picked out and identified everything from the furniture to the linens to the artwork that would complete the puzzle. She even sketched a massive artistic feature wall in the living room. It would be made from two-inch-wide strips of wood mounted to the wall in a custom design that resembled a chevron pattern but had a few extra flairs of creativity sprinkled into it. They called that wall their Insta-moment wall. Dan thought it was odd to hear someone old enough to be his grandmother talk about Instagram, but they've clearly done this before.

"Think about it," Pauline explained. "When someone comes to Hawaii for a month-long vacation, they are going to look for those breathtaking moments every day that they are here. And if you can give them one or two of those moments on your property, then they will advertise for you. So the difference between an amateur and a professional artist often lies in the nuance and their ability to find the right perspective."

Dan's expression told Pauline that he wanted to know more.

THE PERSPECTIVE

She pulled him to the center of the living room, stretched her arms out, made two "Ls" with her hands, and placed one over the other, creating a window to look through, like looking through a camera lens. "See, if you take a picture here. It's okay, but nothing special. But if you take the picture at this angle," Pauline said, as she rotated her body to the left about two feet, now framing a different section of the wall that connected to the sliding glass door leading to the lanai that overlooked the ocean, "Can you see this picture?" Dan nodded. She pulled out her artist pad and flipped to the living room sketch. Dan marveled as he noticed that it was from this exact angle. The perspective was spot on. The feature wall did pull his attention to the right side of the frame, and the design automatically led his eyes out over the lanai and into the ocean. Her sketch showed a sunrise just starting to appear over the horizon.

"It's beautiful!" Dan exclaimed.

Pauline smiled and continued to the bedrooms, sketching out her designs, each one from the perfect perspective.

Dan couldn't help but feel there was a lesson there. An opportunity, a situation, or a property could become something entirely different to different people depending on their perspective, knowledge, expertise, and focus. He was excited to take this thought back to George to see if he could help him work through the idea.

Dan noticed an incoming call from the listing agent for the Makiki home that he was under contract to close on in a week. While he was excited to talk to her and give her the update that everything was back on track for closing, he didn't answer the phone as he wanted to wrap up his time with Bill and Pauline before heading out to start focusing on his purchase. With his *Hail Mary* efforts that led to finding Bill and Pauline and helping them close in record time, Dan had done the impossible to pull in more than enough funds for closing. He had been in contact with his lender, and all was fine. Immediately after receiving a notification that he had a new voicemail, he received a text from the listing agent. *We need to talk. Please call ASAP.*

CHAPTER 17:

The Shift

After reading the text, Dan's heart sank. It sounded urgent. He excused himself and went out onto the lanai to listen to the voicemail.

"Dan, this is Kim. We have a problem. I just got a call from the title attorney. They found an issue with the title, and they cannot get it cleared in time for settlement. There is a tax lien that the seller thought was cleared, but it turns out that it isn't. Dan, it is a big lien, and it involves the seller and a few business partners, so it cannot just be resolved at settlement. The seller's attorney says it will likely take two to three months to resolve, so I don't know what else to say except that the seller can't sell right now. He's also not in a position to leave it vacant for another two to three months. Dan, we need to cancel the contract. The seller needs to rent this out to cover his expenses while resolving his tax lien. I'm so sorry. Please call me so that we can discuss voiding the contract."

Dan played the voicemail again to see if he had heard everything correctly. He did. The seller couldn't sell. His heart sank even further. He thought about calling Kim back right then, but he knew he needed to process the news first. He tapped on the voicemail again to pull up the share options. He opened a new text message to George and attached the voicemail. He also added *Help, please! Would love to discuss this with you.* The message whooshed to confirm it was sent.

Dan did his best to hide his worry when he stepped back into the unit from the lanai. He helped with the last measurements, and as he saw Bill and Pauline start to wrap up, Dan said his goodbyes and headed back to the office.

George was in the training area with a few new agents. They were discussing strategies for a counteroffer. George acknowledged Dan as he walked by and motioned that he would be with him in a moment. "Take your time," Dan replied as he settled into his desk and turned his computer on.

Dan looked at the notes he had written for himself on his whiteboard. His motivation, promises to himself, and the next steps he needed to take for his financial freedom plan--they were all there staring back at him. There was a new message on his board. It was a note from George: *I listened to the voicemail about your Makiki purchase. This is a problem, but there is definitely a solution. It is just a math equation. What creative strategies can you come up with that will allow you to move forward to start with your financial freedom plan on schedule next week? - George.*

Dan read through the message again, and he could feel his worry start to dissipate. There was a solution! Dan would have loved it if George had also written down that solution so he could start working on it, but that was not George's style. He was famous for making his agents and students work through their problems as he knew they could solve them. George felt that the act of problem-solving and creative thinking was where they learned, and he did not want to rob his students of that potential by simply providing them with all the answers. However, this did not feel like a learning moment for Dan. This felt like a *help!* moment.

Dan peeked around the corner and saw that George was still deep in conversation with the other agents. There were also a few phone calls, a training session, and a few conversations he could overhear echoing through the office and making their way back to Dan, preventing him from focusing.

FLOW 2.0: THE ZEN PLAYLIST

Dan decided to put in his noise-canceling air pods and scrolled through his playlists. As part of orientation, George covered a segment on the ability to focus and put yourself in a flow state. He advocated for using music to help you get there. He challenged everyone to create a zen playlist with music that spoke to their soul, which "vibrated at another level," that could put you in a calm and focused state. After a few weeks, Dan found some songs that worked for him, but none better than *Yellow Ledbetter*. Dan found this odd because he wasn't a Pearl Jam fan. He didn't even really understand the lyrics, but he found that it vibrated on a whole different level for him. No matter his mood or stress level, if he zoned out for all five minutes and three seconds of this song, it felt as if he had absorbed its Zen qualities, and everything else melted away. Dan found the song, hit play, and closed his eyes.

After the song ended, he left his noise-canceling earbuds in, stared at his whiteboard, and re-read George's message. *What did he mean by 'it was a math equation?'* Dan wondered. He pulled out a piece of paper and began scribbling notes in a bullet point list format.

What do we know?
- ❖ *The seller wants to sell*
- ❖ *The seller cannot sell right now due to a cloud on the title*
- ❖ *The seller will be able to sell in 3-6 months once the cloud/lien gets cleared up*
- ❖ *The seller cannot carry the property vacant for 3-6 months; thus, they need to rent it out to avoid defaulting on their mortgage*
- ❖ *The contract calls for a void if the seller cannot provide a clear title, so the listing agent is proposing that we void so that the seller can rent it out for a year and sell next year when the tenants move out and the cloud on the title is resolved*

What is the math equation?
- ❖ *The seller has an estimated carrying cost of $3,810 every month for this property.*
- ❖ *The average rent for a property like this is $3,500 a month for a long-term rental*
- ❖ *The landlord has equity in his home but is cash-flow negative by about $300 a month.*
- ❖ *This negative cash-flow seems to be within reason and within the landlord's ability to cover each month.*
- ❖ *My expected expenses once I buy this property are $4,300 a month.*
- ❖ *I plan to bring in a minimum of $4,750 a month by renovating and renting room by room.*
- ❖ *I can afford to pay the landlord higher than market rent if he rents it to me until we can close the purchase, and if he allows me to make*

alterations and sublease to roommates

What are the risks?

- *Landlord/Seller risk: What if the landlord does not like the changes to the property and is stuck with the changes if I end up not buying the property?*

- *Tenant/Buyer risk: What if I spend money to renovate and he decides not to sell? Or cannot sell?*

How would I recoup my costs?

In what ways can I mitigate these risks?

- *First, we can sign a lease with the option to buy. This will lock in the purchase agreement option for me while also assuring the seller that I intend to purchase the property at the price for which we are under contract.*

- *We can build in a $15,000 penalty if I do not buy the property. This protects the seller from their worries about allowing me to make alterations to the property.*

- *Finally, we can build in a $15,000 penalty if the seller cannot clear the cloud to sell to me. This would protect me as the purchaser and allow me to recoup the costs that I put into renovating the property.*

THE LEASE OPTION

Dan looked at his list and tried to see any gaps. It seemed to cover all angles. He drafted up a lease with the option to buy. The lease would be $3,810 a month, which was above market rent and covered the landlord/seller's carrying costs. This higher than market value rent would come with the stipulation that Dan had permission to paint, renovate, and sublease rooms as he saw fit. There would be an agreement of sale at the same price they were under contract to sell right now, but it extended the closing date to the earliest point possible, within the next twelve months. A $15,000 option deposit would be put in escrow, which would go to the seller if Dan defaulted and did not buy the property. If Dan purchased the property, the $15,000 would go towards his down payment. He also included a $15,000 penalty to the seller if the seller could not clear the title within the next twelve months and could not sell it. This would protect Dan to recoup any money he spent fixing up the property.

Dan called Kim and explained his proposal. She was not familiar with a lease option and was skeptical, but that didn't deter Dan. He sent her the signed offer and a detailed description. He also recorded a screen-capture video that broke down every section of the offer.

Kim called Dan back a few hours later to say that the seller was open to the offer terms but did not want to commit to a $15,000 penalty if he couldn't sell. Dan re-ran the numbers, and after a little back and forth, they settled on a three-year lease option term with no penalty to the seller. Dan knew that even in a worst-case scenario, if the seller could not sell, having a three-year lease meant he would be able to live for free for three years and make a profit every month. So, they made the changes and ratified the new contract terms.

Exhale.

Step number one, complete.

CHAPTER 18:

The Butter Mochi

"It's been a whirlwind," Dan said to the newest Breakfast Club member. Josh was a twenty-one-year-old college kid that had the same deer in the headlights look that Dan suspected he had when he attended his first Breakfast Club meeting just over eight months ago. "I have been attending these groups for less than a year, and it feels like we have covered ten years of content. I wish I knew about this group, or real estate investing in general when I was twenty-one," Dan said.

"I'm pretty excited," Josh replied enthusiastically. "It's my dream to be a musician. My dad was a musician my whole life, and it's the one thing that I live for. I love playing at coffee shops and restaurants on the weekend. My dad understands the passion and the need I have to be out playing, but he also saw the financial strain that inconsistent income caused for my mom and our family. So, when I was still in middle school, my dad made me promise that I would only pursue music as a hobby and side gig until I was retired or set financially. He knew that jumping in full-time in the beginning would likely lead to the same stress and heartache that he put his family through. I can't imagine doing anything for a living other than playing music. I have worked as a barista, a waiter, and in an office. Everything I do feels like a lie if I'm not playing music. I am a musician. That is who I am. So, getting a job and working for thirty or forty years until I could retire did not seem like an option that I could live with. This year, I became obsessed with real estate as a vehicle for passive income and retirement, and I ended up being referred to George," Josh said, pausing, not knowing if he was sharing too much.

Dan smiled. "Don't worry. We share everything in this group. You will get used to it," he said as he looked around the room at his fellow Breakfast Club members. "I am a very private person, but somehow, this group changes you. In just eight months, they have become my family."

Just then, Dan felt a squeeze and a hug from behind him. The hairs on his arms stood up a little as he detected the aroma of vanilla bean. It was Sarah.

"Almost family," she said with a big smile.

Dan put his arm around Sarah and turned back to Josh. "Josh, meet my fiancée, Sarah."

Sarah, still hugging Dan from the side, started to chat with Josh. Dan watched his fiancée, mesmerized by her command of the room and the conversation. *What a whirlwind indeed!* Dan thought contentedly. The last eight months had been the best eight months of his real estate career. He had an intensity, focus, and passion that he has never had before. He made it a daily practice to put himself in a flow state every morning and sometimes multiple times a day. His previously inconsistent real estate income was now very consistent, and he was able to hire his first full-time assistant and buyer's agent. These two team members allowed him to focus more time on the CEO-related activities for his business as he delegated more of the day-to-day work to them. He had to pivot multiple times to make step number one work, which was getting rid of his housing expenses. Although he didn't own it yet, his house hack allowed him to live for free and bring in passive income. It turned out that he could raise his per-room rent when he started offering perks like free house cleaning, free internet, and free streaming services. After he moved in, he dedicated the first three weeks to the renovations and could pre-market the rooms for rent. He was overwhelmed with applications. He started with six-month agreements that moved to month-to-month after that. He thought about doing year-long leases, but he didn't want to be stuck with a roommate for a year that wasn't a good fit for the house.

Once he settled in, Sarah offered to help him with step number two, which was hiding his new cash-flow from himself -#IgnoreThe-Joneses. During their lunch break one day, Sarah made a trip to the bank with Dan. She explained to the bank manager that they wanted access to his accounts online along with a separate account that could receive transferred funds from the other accounts every month, but this account would not be visible to Dan when he checked his account balances online. Sarah did all the talking for Dan at the bank meeting, so the bank manager mistook her for being Dan's wife and referred to her as Mrs. Carter multiple times. Dan felt like his face went white the first time the bank manager made the mistake. He was about to correct him when Sarah smiled, squeezed Dan's arm, and referred to him as *honey*. She was tickled with the pretend role she was just offered and ran with it. By the end of the meeting, she pinched Dan's cheeks and referred to him as *hubby*. Still nervous and embarrassed, Dan didn't say more than a few words for the rest of their time at the bank. He let his pretend wife take charge and get everything set up for him. They left the bank arm in arm and burst into laughter the moment they walked out.

"Well, honey? It was great getting to play Mrs. Carter today," Sarah said, clearly still tickled.

"It suited you well," Dan replied.

The moment he said it, he panicked. *What did that even mean?*

Sarah raised her eyebrow, impressed with his bold comeback. "I love your confidence, but I think you'd have to at least buy me dinner first." She was waiting for Dan's reaction. It was like playing a game of chess. Check.

Dan's heart began to beat out of his chest. He took a deep breath and responded with, "Okay then, I'm free tonight. You?" Check.

"It's a date," she said with slightly wide eyes. Checkmate.

They chatted a little more, then she hugged him and returned to work. *And the rest is history*, Dan thought, still smiling at Sarah as she spoke with Josh.

Dan's Makiki property and situation had become somewhat of a case study for the group. Each class, Dan shared an update, and he even had George and a handful of the group members walk through as he was finishing up the renovations. George was proud of the creative solutions Dan came up with and happy with his ability to pivot his plan as he met obstacles along the way.

During one of these walk-throughs, a group member asked what Dan and Sarah would do about their living situation once they got married. Dan had put some thought into this, but he and Sarah had not discussed it in depth yet. It didn't make sense to give up this house hack right away as he needed to see the benefits of living without a housing payment for a few years to progress with his financial freedom plan. However, the suggestion was made to figure out a way to reduce the number of roommates without reducing the rent. The easiest change was to section off the downstairs area and turn it into a separate living area since it had its own entrance already. Dan decided to add a kitchenette downstairs and put up a door at the bottom of the stairs, allowing him to separate the downstairs space from the rest of the house.

Dan connected with Bill and Pauline and learned everything he could about vacation rentals. Pauline was excited for Dan and walked him through the now two-bedroom, one-bath unit. She even sketched out a design that she knew would wow his guests. As she did for every one of their units before, Pauline drew visual masterpieces for each room, and Dan followed those blueprints to a T. In all, Dan spent another $20,000 renovating and furnishing the downstairs unit, but, rather than bringing in $1,100 a month for each of the two rooms, he was now getting anywhere between $175 to $250 a night with a one-week minimum stay. Thanks to Pauline's brilliant design inspiration and Dan's marketing skills, the downstairs unit was booked out solid for six months. With a $210 a night average, and guests paying a separate cleaning fee, Dan was now netting close to $5,000 a month on the downstairs unit instead of the $2,200 that he was getting before. Added to the three separate room rentals upstairs, Dan brought in $8,300 a month in rent. After paying all his expenses, he was now living for free and making a profit of $3,390 every month. His goal was to bring in enough income from the unit downstairs to allow him and Sarah to have the upper two floors, which would give them a four-bedroom, three-bath unit all to themselves once they were ready to move in together. Sarah liked the plan but insisted that they keep renting out the upper three units, ideally to friends, for as long as possible, while she and Dan occupied the main level master bedroom. She knew at some point they would outgrow their situation and would need more space, especially once they had children, but until then, she did not want to disrupt the financial freedom plan.

With George's help, Dan reworked his plan to reflect his current situation. He was hiding $4,300 from himself every month, as that was the amount he would eventually be paying for his mortgage and expenses, even though he was currently paying less for his rent. That totaled up to $51,600 a year that he was setting aside now that he had gotten rid of his housing expenses. However, now that he had $3,390 a month of additional income, he put all of it away into his investment down payment account, which was $92,280 a year saved.

Dan marveled at that number. Never in his life, no matter how great of a year he had income-wise, had he ever been able to save $92,280. Now he would be doing that every year without feeling a pinch at all. In two years, once he completed his debt snowball payoff, he would have an additional $43,200 a year that he would have to put towards his financial freedom investments. Aside from this, his real estate business was now thriving, and he could put some of those profits aside, too, if he wanted.

Dan's house hack Breakdown

- Makiki house 5 bed 3.5 bath. Contract to purchase at $750k
- 5% down ($37,500) cost when purchased
- 3-year lease option at $3810/mo (above market rent. Covers sellers PITI)
- Spent $15k + sweat equity to convert to 6 bed 4 bath
- Spent additional $20k to reno/furnish the lower level for Airbnb
- Total out of pocket: $72,500 (after purchase)
- Lives in newly created main level master suite (for free)
- Rents upstairs rooms at $1050-$1200/mo (provides free internet, streaming & cleaning service)
- Rents downstairs for $175-$250/night ($210/night average) for approx. $5000/mo
- Total rents = $8300 a month
- Total expenses = $4910 a month which includes $3810 rent + $200 for internet and streaming services + $500 for utilities + $400 for cleaning services
- Dan lives for free (saving him $4300/mo) + makes $3390/mo
- Dan hides $7690 from himself every month = $92,280/year for investing
- After 2 years once he is debt-free he will add $43,200 a year for a total of $135,480 for investing every year.

Just over two months earlier, Dan was presented with an opportunity to jump into step number three and buy his first cash-flow rental property. The landlord that Julie was buying her property from told her that he had a four-plex next door he was thinking about selling and asked her if she wanted to buy it. Julie felt it was too soon for her to buy her next property, but she ran the numbers through George's financial freedom cash-flow calculator, and it more than met the minimum requirements for Dan's first property. She called Dan up and asked if he wanted to be a landlord and neighbor to her.

It felt weird for Dan to consider buying a rental property before he owned his own home. Still, after consulting with George and verifying that the math worked out, he decided to move forward with the offer on the rental property. Julie called the landlord back and said that although she couldn't buy it, her brother could. Once they agreed on the terms verbally, she reached out to her real estate agent and lender so they could begin working with Dan to put the deal in writing. The process took off from there. Dan was impressed by the efficiency and speed with which the broker and lender could put the deal together and coordinate the inspections, surveys, appraisals, and walk-throughs. *Is this what it's like when you work with investor-focused real estate agents?* They understood what was important and what was not. They educated and guided Dan on the market and area, helped him understand what to look at, and helped decipher the inspection report through an investor's versus a consumer's eyes.

"Every problem has a number. So, if we could figure out what number to assign to each item, you can plug it into your equation to make sure it still makes sense as an investment," his real estate agent explained.

After the inspection, they were able to get the seller to take care of all the deferred maintenance on the property. Since this was an off-market deal, the seller knew he was saving a lot of time and money not having to get his home ready for the market, so he was agreeable to a closing cost credit to the buyer to help reduce Dan's out-of-pocket expenses. Dan spoke with his lender, and she explained that for the conventional investor loan he was getting, the maximum allowable seller credit would be 2% of the purchase price, so they wrote that into the contract. This covered almost all of Dan's closing costs. After all negotiations were completed, he brought just under $100,000 to the table, a 25% down payment on a roughly $400,000 property. Because it exceeded the 1.25% rule, after paying PITI and OpEx/CapEx, he had a PIFL of about $2,000 every month or $24,000 a year.

Dan was amazed, as the numbers penciled out even better than his target first property's minimum requirements in his plan. This was a 24% Cash on Cash ROI deal. That was before Dan even started to consider automatic equity gained through debt reduction by the tenants paying for his mortgage every month, the tax savings to offset other gains through depreciation, and the potential appreciation in value due to market conditions. Dan did the quick math George taught him, which looked at the overall return of the deal. Assuming the market stayed on track and was identical to the year before, he would see a 52.3% return in his first year after factoring in all "wealth triggers," as George would call them.

Even if the market was flat and there was zero appreciation the first year he owned it, he would see a 32% return based on cash-flow, debt reduction, and tax savings through depreciation. *Not bad for my first investment.*

Once Dan received his first set of rent payments, paid the mortgage, and set aside the reserves, he set up an automatic monthly transfer of $2,000 PIFL to his hidden account to be added to the house hacking money he would use in a year to buy his next property.

Dan refocused his attention on Sarah as she wrapped up her conversation with Josh. He reached for her hand as they took their usual seats at the back of the classroom in anticipation of George starting the meeting. Just as the clock hit 7 p.m., George turned down the music, indicating that networking time was over and that the Breakfast Club meeting would be starting soon. He was speaking with Julie in the corner of the conference room. Dan tried to make out what they were discussing. From afar, it seemed like he was providing her with some additional words of wisdom before she left on a long journey. Finally, he hugged her. As she left the room, he turned to the group and motioned for everyone to take a seat to get started. Moments later, Julie re-entered the room with a massive cookie sheet stacked high with butter mochi. The room quickly took notice, and there were cheers from the group. She was beaming ear to ear as she placed it on one of the high-top conference tables and told the group to help themselves.

George paused to let Julie make it back up to the front. "That takes us to our first order of business," he said. "The butter mochi is likely a dead giveaway for most of you, but today Julie will be ringing the gong!"

The group erupted with cheers and applause. After about a minute straight of applause and a few moments where Julie was trying to control her emotions, she raised her hand to show she was ready to speak. Dan felt tears start to well up in his eyes as he watched his sister with pride. He looked around the room. He knew that everyone there saw Julie as a sister, too. They were all just as proud and happy for her as he was. They all knew her story and experienced her highs and lows with her along the way. Now that she had closed on and stabilized her most recent multifamily property, she had finally hit her financial freedom number. Her passive income now exceeded her expenses by about $1,000 every month. If she wanted to, she could retire at the age of 32. But that is not what she was going to do. This moment meant that she could continue to do what she loved, which was teaching, but without the stress, guilt, or internal conflict she had from working in a profession that did not meet her financial needs. Her financial requirements were met regardless of the money she made teaching now. *What an achievement!* Dan thought.

Julie began to tell her story from the beginning. George would always ask this of his students when they achieved milestones. "We all have stories," George would say. "Most of us don't know where our story is going. But in this group, our stories are intentional. We share our stories as it reminds us of the path that we are on, and it inspires others who are on that path as well."

CHAPTER 19:

The Flags We Wave

Dan watched his sister share her milestones, stories he had heard many times before, ones he had been a part of. George, too, was beaming with pride as he listened to Julie recount her story and her numbers with precision. Dan had made it a habit of referring to George as his mentor, but at that moment, he looked at Julie and couldn't help but realize his younger sister had been a mentor to him, too. Dan turned to Sarah, whose hand he was still holding, and realized that she had also been his mentor. He went down the list of group members in his mind, and everyone, no matter how new or experienced they were, played their role. Was this the magic that Julie referred to during orientation? Although George clearly provided the initial knowledge and training, that knowledge spread through the group like blood circulates through every organ and limb of the body, eventually taking on a life of its own. Knowledge becomes experience for one student. That experience becomes new knowledge for the other students as stories are shared, and everyone learns from their fellow group members. Learn something, implement it, experience it, then teach it to someone else. That was the standard that they were all held to. It was about taking the solo investor's journey and putting it in an incubator or a pressure cooker of sorts, and then fast-tracking their learning curve and evolution of ideas as the group experienced the stories of hundreds of investment projects together. That was the magic of the group.

Julie completely changed Dan's idea of who an investor was. Before this group, he thought of investors as men in suits, faceless entities, corporate conglomerates trying to absorb or devour everything in their path.

They were sure as heck not schoolteachers, single moms, hotel staff, or college students.

Dan recalled mentioning this to Julie several months ago, which led to a long discussion about their upbringing, the imprint that communities have on who people become and the ideas they have. "Think about it. Dan," he remembers Julie saying. "Growing up Hawaiian, in Hawaii, we have a lot to be grateful for. However, as you know, there is an underlying tone of oppression, hurt, and need for restitution that is just a part of who we are because of the history of our ancestors and what was done to them. This is what I teach in school, and I know that history is important. But the anger and hurt that still comes up in so many of those from our culture around the topic of the United States overthrowing the Kingdom of Hawaii in the late 1800s is intense. One day we had a queen, and the next day, against our will, our entire government, our entire country was swallowed up by this faceless outside entity called America," Julie said. Dan had versions of this conversation with Julie many times before. All their lives, Julie was very passionate about this topic and would always get worked up when discussing it. However, this time she seemed calmer. More at peace.

"Once America took over, there was a strategic effort to erase our culture, and they did this by forbidding Hawaiian to be spoken or written in schools. It only took one generation of strict enforcement in schools to kill our language and nearly wipe out the essence of our culture. I used to get so mad about this. It happened over a hundred and twenty years ago, but it's still affecting the trajectory of my life. I debated this topic with George several times over the last few years, but it finally clicked for me at one of our regular check-ins about two years ago. He sat me down because he saw my anger and my frustration. He saw that my upset led to my distrust, and this identity of distrust, of being a victim, conflicted with everything that George taught us in the Breakfast Club. My mantra was 'we deserve restitution,' but George preached that 'no one owes us anything. We are entitled to nothing. Never be a victim of our circumstances. Go out and create everything that you want for your life. Don't wait for someone to give it to you.' As you can expect, I objected early and often. I was that problem child in class, always trying to carve out an exception for my situation and my pain. Remember when grandma made sure all of us registered to enter the Hawaiian Homes Homestead land program? As you know, it's a program the United States created as a form of restitution to the Hawaiian people. It was seen as a huge victory when they introduced it in the 1920s. All you had to do as a native Hawaiian was register, and if they picked your name from the lottery, you would have the right to lease land for a dollar a year! What a gift!" Dan still remembered the sarcasm in Julie's voice when she said this.

DON'T WASTE PAIN

Julie continued. "At this coffee meeting with George, he asked me to make a list of everyone I knew that had put their name on that list, so I did that. I came up with about eighteen. He then told me to circle the people who were awarded a lease. I circled zero names. He then asked me to underline the people on the list who owned real estate or did any sort of investing. There were only two. George demonstrated that this 'gift,' or this 'restitution' held us back. It reinforced the victim mentality, which has a way of stopping most people from taking control, or taking ownership of their lives and outcomes, because they are waiting for what is owed to them.

George said that bad things happen to everyone, some more than others. It is a part of life. It is a part of the existence and experience that we were given. And to many, it is easy to say it's not fair and to suggest that we should all have equal experiences. But that will never be the case. There is nothing we can do about that. The only thing we can do is control how we experience, react to, and control our existence with intention. George looked me in the eyes and said in the most serious tone that I have ever heard from him, 'Never let anything that happens to you control you. You always have a choice. You can't choose what happens to you, but you can choose how you use that experience, that situation, that pain to get to where you want to go, to create what you want to create.'

I remember George pausing and finishing with a comment that struck me to my core. 'The most wasted resource of all time is pain. Never let your pain go to waste.' And just like that, our coffee meeting was over. I was stuck with a storm of conflicting thoughts and emotions. It was eye-opening to realize how many people we know, our friends, our family, myself, put their lives and future on hold, refusing to buy their own homes because they were waiting to be picked. They were waiting to get what they were entitled to. Dan, I cried. I cried for days.

I barely got out of bed for three days. At first, I was devastated because I felt like my life, my identity was a lie. I knew that I didn't want to be a victim anymore, but that was who I was for so long. Was I giving up my Hawaiian culture or letting my ancestors down somehow by letting this anger go? Then I cried because I thought of all the people I influenced to wave a victim flag with me. How many of those people will never fully take ownership or control of their future and destiny because of my mentality?

Then about three days into this self-pity party, I stopped crying. I decided then and there never to be a victim again. I needed to take control of my own destiny. I needed to plan out my future and not wait for anyone to hand anything to me. I took my name off the list. I vowed never to take a handout again. I vowed never to take restitution again. My mantra became, 'No one owes me anything!' I wrote this in my journal every morning like some insane person. I did this over and over and over again, until one day, this became my new identity. I became more passionate about this belief and cause than the opposing victim and entitled mindset that had previously consumed me. That is why I wanted to fast-track through my financial freedom plan, to get there so that I can start teaching and spreading this mentality to the people that I love, the people that may be putting their lives and future on hold because of the victim flag that I gave them."

Dan remembered feeling conflicted after this conversation with Julie. Growing up, he was never as passionate about Hawaiian sovereignty and restitution as Julie was, but he also signed up to receive a handout if and when they pulled his name from the hat. However, after their talk, Dan decided to make the same commitments she did, to take one hundred percent ownership of his life, of what he achieved or didn't.

At this meeting, Dan realized that investors weren't just faceless entities or emotionless corporate conglomerates. They were sisters, single moms, hotel workers, college students, and real estate agents who had committed one hundred percent ownership--no excuses, no handouts. They were people that had figured out a way to be intentional with their financial future. They were people who understood they could not trust their financial future to any one person, employer, organization, or government. It was on each person to make it happen for themselves.

Dan came back to the present when he heard his name as part of Julie's story. It was getting to the end. Dan, an opposing force at the beginning of her story, was now an advocate, a partner in the final chapter of her financial freedom book. The group gave Julie another standing ovation that seemed to go on forever as she rang the gong. *More butter mochi, please.*

As the networking portion started to wind down, the group thinned out until there were only four: Dan, George, Julie, and Sarah. It was as if none of them wanted the day to end. They worked together to rearrange chairs and furniture back to their regular layout and get the room ready for work the following day. George excused himself, then he reappeared from the direction of his office a few minutes later with a few small envelopes in hand. He moved to the center where the three remaining Breakfast Club members were putting the final touches on their cleanup effort. He stood there for a few seconds, reading the label on each envelope.

"Julie, I am extremely proud of you for completing your financial freedom plan," George said. "Dan and Sarah, I am proud of each of you as well, as you are focused and well on your path to financial freedom and will be achieving it far sooner than either of you initially planned for."

Sarah smiled and exchanged a look with Dan as they had spoken a few times about combining their financial freedom plans into one once they were married. The quick math showed them that doubling their income but not their expenses could super-charge their plans and get them to financial freedom in just over two years. Dan planned to run the math by George right after Julie's Breakfast Club graduation.

George handed Julie a bluish-teal envelope with her name written on the front in gold. "Think of this as a graduation gift and an invitation to a higher level of education. A higher level of investing. A higher level of purpose. Earlier I alluded to financial freedom being your half marathon. Well, this is your invitation to the full marathon. He turned to Dan and Sarah and handed them identical envelopes. I am supposed to wait to give these to you until you each ring the gong. However, I think the three of you could do amazing things in this group if you grow together, help each other make an impact, and push each other to grow and thrive. Dan and Sarah, if you choose to become members of this new group, that would be a commitment in addition to that of your

Breakfast Club commitment." George appeared to look them deeper in the eye to see if they grasped the importance of the moment. Both Dan and Sarah nodded.

"Good," George said. "The information in these invitations is very time-sensitive, so please review them together tonight." With that, George hugged each of them and left.

"What just happened?" Dan asked, mainly to break the silence.

"I know what this is," Julie said with a chuckle. "I thought I was graduating with a master's degree in real estate investing, and George just reminded us that we are still in kindergarten."

Julie broke the seal on her envelope and folded back the teal flap, exposing an intricately embossed card. She slid it out of the envelope with equal parts awe and excitement as her audience waited in anticipation. The card rivaled some of the best wedding invitations she had ever seen. It was all black with gold and silver lettering at the top that read, *You are invited to become a member of the Legacy Dinner Club, where real estate investing fuels your purpose.* On the back of the card a longer description appeared: *The Legacy Dinner Club is not for everyone, and you may decide that it is not for you, and that is okay. This Dinner Club is not about making more money. The Dinner Club is about building something much bigger than yourself. It is about building to a level of success far beyond your needs with the sole purpose of being able to give it away. It is the level of legacy and generational wealth where you turn your passion into your purpose, and you build something that can be seen from space--something that will impact this world far beyond your time here. This will become a lifelong journey. Are you ready for it?"* At the bottom it read, *If this excites you, and if you accept this challenge, meet me at my second office tomorrow at 7 a.m.*

"Of course, his dinner club would meet at 7 a.m.," Dan chuckled.

Dan and Sarah opened their cards to find identical invitations. The three of them stood there in silence, somewhat in shock.

"How much more could there be?" Dan asked. There was no response.

They were all deep in thought, contemplating the level of commitment they would be willing to make. The three of them left without discussing whether they would be seeing each other at the meeting following morning. They knew each of them had to make their own commitment. Or maybe they didn't want to ask the others because they hadn't yet decided what their own answer would be.

CHAPTER 20:

The Legacy Dinner Club

Dan pulled up to Like-Like Drive Inn at 6:50 a.m. He scanned the parking lot and saw Julie's car, but he didn't see Sarah's. He was worried about this. *What if one of us wanted to go down this path, but the other didn't? How would we be able to manage that as a couple?*

Dan contemplated going home. He read through his invitation again. The words were embossed, some raised, some indented. He closed his eyes and ran his fingers across each word, visualizing them. There was so much meaning here. There was a purpose beyond self. Ever since reading the words on the invitation the night before, he couldn't help but feel a yearning to identify his bigger purpose in this world.

He woke up at 2:48 a.m. the night before and started to make a list of things that he would want to do if he were financially free. What would he build? What would he do? Who could he impact? He came up with a list that spanned two pages. Some of it was self, some of it was family, some of it was community, and some of it was humanity in general. Dan grew up in a very charitable household, and they were taught at a young age to give as much of their time and money to charity as they could. Dan always felt the importance of this as he saw how many people were impacted when they gave back.

He remembered going as a young boy with his grandfather, his dad, his brothers, and a few people from their church and scouting groups to help rebuild homes devastated in the category-four hurricane Iniki in the early nineties. Although it caused damage on all the islands, it damaged Kauai the most. Iniki completely destroyed over fourteen-hundred homes and damaged over five thousand.

Dan's family and friends volunteered their time and resources to help rebuild as many homes as they could over the next few months. There were many smaller causes and charities that they took part in, but nothing as big or impactful as what they did that summer. He remembered his parents volunteering a lot of their time, but when it came to donating money, they would often say, "If we had more, we would give more." They never quite got to the "having more" phase, so they continued to help in the ways they could, even though money was always tight.

Dan recalled repeating the same phrase to his mom one day, "When I have more, I will give more," when discussing his inability to contribute to a local cause that she was championing. For the first time, with his financial freedom plan, Dan felt a sense of calm and security. Although he was not there yet, he found it easier to tithe, to contribute financially to causes that were important to him. The thought of being able to supercharge those causes and donations, or even starting his own foundation excited him as he reread through his list that morning.

With his eyes still closed, Dan's fingers got to the end of the embossed lettering. This was it. Dan felt deep down in his bones that he wanted to commit to this. He put the card down and checked the time. 6:58 a.m. One quick scan of the parking lot again. No trace of Sarah.

He took a deep breath, got out of his car, and walked into the restaurant. Just then, his watch buzzed to notify him of an incoming text. It was from Sarah. *I see you in your car. Are you coming in?* Smiley face emoji, heart emoji. Dan looked up and caught Sarah arm in arm with Julie. *Of course, they rode together*, Dan laughed to himself. He was relieved. He couldn't wait to be able to take this journey with her.

He gave both Sarah and Julie a hug, then surveyed the room. It was a smaller group than the Breakfast Club with only around fifteen people. George made eye contact with Dan and gave him a nod of approval. George checked his watch. 7 a.m. He motioned for everyone to take a seat. The group occupied six booths, three on the left and three on the right. George stood between the two rows in the aisle. With this being his second office, it was clear that the restaurant staff welcomed him, and gave him an entire wing so that they could meet there every month uninterrupted. No digital whiteboard in sight, George propped open an easel with a big flip chart, turned to the first blank page, and wrote: *Welcome to the Legacy Dinner Club!*

George turned to the group and announced that their first order of business was to welcome the three newest members to the club. He pointed at Dan's booth, where he was sitting with Sarah and Julie. He introduced them by name and encouraged the group to get to know them during the networking portion.

The 3 Types of Real Estate Investors

1. **Investor as a profession:** Full-time, Part-time or Hobbyist - Doing it for active income or supplemental income to spend now.
   - Feeds/Satisfies their Curiosity (creative outlet)

2. **Financial Freedom Investor:** 100% focus on increasing passive income to exceed expenses.
   - Funds their Passion

3. **Generational Wealth or Legacy investor:** Already financially free but wants to grow, build or do something bigger.
   - Fuels their Purpose

THE 3 TYPES OF REAL ESTATE INVESTORS

George continued. "Since we have new members today, let's spend our first few minutes covering some of the basics."

He flipped his chart to the next page and wrote,

The three types of investors:

1. Curiosity
2. Passion
3. Purpose

"There are countless types of real estate investments, but you can generally break down most of them into one of three categories.

The first category, or phase one investor, is the investor as a profession. This can be a full-time investor, part-time, or hobbyist, but in any case, they are doing it for active or supplemental income that they plan to use now. This feeds their curiosity, and they use it either for active income, as a creative outlet, or both. Most clients that come to me who want to learn how to start investing in real estate would usually fall into this category initially.

The second category, or phase two investor, is the financial freedom investor. This type of investor focuses one hundred percent on using real estate investing to increase their passive income until it exceeds their living expenses. This track funds your passion. It doesn't matter if you are passionate about spending more time with family, traveling the world, or your work. Achieving financial freedom gives you the choices, the options, and of course, the freedom to do what you want and to follow your passion. Our Cash-flow Breakfast Club focuses on this investor. Once again, an investor is only in this phase or mode for a set period, usually two to seven years. Most hit their financial freedom goals in five years. Then, once you have financial independence, you can retire, continue to work and increase your financial freedom position, or shift and start looking at building something beyond you," George said as he scanned the room.

"That brings us to the third and final category, or phase three investor, the generational wealth or legacy investor. Too many people make the mistake of jumping into this category before they are financially free. That is like wanting to do gymnastics before learning to walk. So many people crash and burn in the process because they do not have the correct foundation. During phase three, an investor can chase their passions because they are financially free to do so. Your passion is self. Your passion is inward-focused: your family, friends, hobbies, travel, interests, and so on. However, at some point you have the opportunity to focus that passion outward and evolve it into a greater purpose than you. This type of investor reaches a point where they become obsessed with growth to give back. They want to grow beyond where they actually need to grow. They want to build more, do more, and become more. The more they build, the more they grow, the more it fuels their purpose, and the greater the legacy they can leave. You can have a family-focused legacy, a community-focused legacy, a globally-focused legacy, or a combination of all three."

Dan saw heads nodding in agreement as George spoke. This was not the first time that they had heard this sermon. They likely went over this every time a new member joined.

Dan did not know what his purpose was. He wanted to have a greater purpose but felt stuck. He loved real estate. He loved helping people. But ever since he learned the difference between a real estate investor and a real estate consumer, he felt guilty just helping people buy and sell homes without educating them on the world of real estate investing. It wasn't about picking them up as investor clients. None of that seemed to matter anymore. He felt like he had been in a fog his whole life, and he could see clearly for the first time. *Everyone needs to know about this! Could this be my purpose? Am I supposed to help as many people as possible down this same path?* He thought it through a little more but could not think of anything that he could do that would change more lives and make a more significant impact. *That's it. I need to become the best investor that I can be, so that one day I can continue George's work, amplify his reach to as many new investors as possible, and teach them the path that I was given. Every new investor I coach might become their own ripple in the pond, expanding, blessing, and positively impacting as many lives as they possibly can in the process.*

Dan felt like he had made a breakthrough and was excited to discuss it with Sarah. He jotted down a few quick notes to remember his inspiration, and then turned back to George's training.

GROW, IMPACT, THRIVE

"See, without a purpose," George continued, "all of us reach a limit. Every successful investor, at some point, will get to a place where it simply doesn't make sense for them to buy another property or do another deal. And once it stops mattering, your motivation and growth stop as well. However, that is where purpose comes in. Your purpose is like a fishbowl to a goldfish. Just like the size that a goldfish will grow is directly related to the size of the fish tank you put it in, the size of your purpose will limit your growth in real estate investing. The larger the fish tank, the larger the goldfish grows. Likewise, the larger your purpose is, the greater your why is, the larger your potential to expand as a real estate investor is.

"Our focus, our motto as a group is to grow, impact and thrive. We each commit to grow. Grow our knowledge, grow our portfolio, and grow our tribe of financially free real estate investors. That way, we can work together to positively impact our communities either on a family, community, or global scale, and provide the knowledge, resources, and tools for the next generations to thrive," George said.

"Now, if that doesn't get you fired up, I don't know what will," said a man in one of the booths across from Dan. Some others in the group nodded, and so did George, welcoming the participation. He was an older gentleman with gray hair, dark skin, and piercing dark eyes. Dan had noticed his plain attire--a t-shirt and surf shorts—earlier that morning. There was an air of confidence and a presence of calm about him, much like about George.

ALL INCOME IS NOT CREATED EQUAL

George walked over to the man, put his hand on his shoulder, and turned to the group. "Most of you know my mentor, Kimo. He was the one who taught me the core principles about real estate investing that eventually changed my life." This took Dan and Julie by surprise, and they turned to get a better look at Kimo as George spoke.

"Starting out, I was stubborn," George said as he turned towards his mentor, who acknowledged the comment with a smile. "Kimo was the one who showed me that all income was not created equal. I had a hard time understanding and accepting this concept. He got very detailed about trading your time for money versus having money come in without trading your time. He also broke down the differences in how different types of income are taxed. Once I got this concept, everything changed for me. Once you buy back your time and leverage the different tax saving structures that are tied to passive income versus earned income, it turns out that passive or created income is worth about ten times as much as active or earned income. So, $1,000 of passive or created income a month is worth $10,000 of active or earned income a month. $10,000 of passive income is worth $100,000 of active income. $100,000 of passive income is worth $1,000,000 of active income. It clicked for me and led to my quest. This started my obsession of perfecting the path towards passive income and financial freedom," George said.

"You see, the financial freedom track is all about sacrifice for a set period. The real fun starts after financial freedom. The real fun starts in this group as we build a legacy and create generational wealth. Once you are financially free, it now makes sense that you can take higher risks for higher rewards. You can hui or partner up with other like-minded members to tackle projects together. Here is a list of the projects that many of you are working on together," George said as he turned his flip chart revealing a handwritten graph of twenty-four projects. Dan read through the list of addresses, dollar amounts, and descriptions, most of which he had no clue about.

Dan raised his hand and asked George what one of the descriptions meant. "What does BRRRR mean?" he asked.

"Ah, there is a great book by David Greene that covers this in detail. It is a concept that has been around in commercial and residential real estate for as long as debt financing has been around. But Brandon Turner, the host of the Bigger Pockets podcast, put a framework around it and brilliantly coined the term. BRRRR stands for Buy, Rehab, Rent, Refinance, Repeat." George turned to his list and pointed out the active projects that were BRRRRs. "Out of these twenty-four active projects that are going on in this group, it looks like seventeen are at some point in the BRRRR process. Take project number eight, for example. We just completed the refinance on this yesterday, so it has completed the full BRRRR cycle. Five members of this group created a hui and did this project together," George explained. He turned to Kimo and asked if he would be willing to break down the project and numbers for the group.

Kimo nodded and pulled out a notepad to review his notes. "George, Maureen, Sam, Paul, and I partnered on this small BRRRR deal together," Kimo said as he looked around the room, making eye contact with and acknowledging each member of his hui. "George's Northern Virginia area broker found a deal in Winchester, Virginia, about 90 minutes outside of DC. We purchased a vacant duplex on the MLS with potential structural issues. Because of the structural concerns, there wasn't a ton of competition for this property, and we were able to negotiate the price down to about $130,000 cash. Our contractors could determine that it wasn't a structural issue, instead just a few rotten joists in one back room. That reduced a potential major problem down to about a $3,000 fix. All in, we spent about $25,000 on the repairs and renovations of this property. We salvaged the hardwood floors and refinished them where we could, and then we added new laminate wood flooring and new tile elsewhere. We moved a few walls around, allowing us to convert unit A from a 1-bedroom unit to a 2-bedroom unit, and unit B from a 2-bedroom unit to a 3-bedroom unit. New bathroom vanities, new paint and new appliances finished this off to become the nicest rental on the block. With permitting, the process took about three months," Kimo said.

"We had our broker put them both on the market for rent at the same time, and we received twenty-eight applications in total. We found two amazing sets of long-term tenants, and now the duplex is renting for between $1400-$1500 a unit for a total of $2975 a month total. Once we had seasoned the property for six months, we started the refinance process. Last week the appraisal came back at just over $300,000, which is exactly what we estimated it to be. So, in six months, by spending $25,000 on the right type of property improvements, we created over $170,000 of added value. The bank allowed us to refinance 75% of the new appraisal value, which was $225,000. After lender closing costs, we got a check for approximately $215,000. So, in summary, each member put in anywhere between $10,000 to $60,000 for varying ownership stakes in the LLC and deal. Now that the BRRRR is complete, each member has received their invested funds back, and as a group, we have over $60,000 of tax-free gains. And we own a renovated duplex that, after paying the mortgage, taxes, insurance, property manager and setting aside funds for reserves, brings in about $1200 a month PIFL for the group. Since we have none of our own money left in the deal, that is now an infinite return on investment. Now we are looking for similar deals to roll those tax-free gains and rental income into to repeat the process."

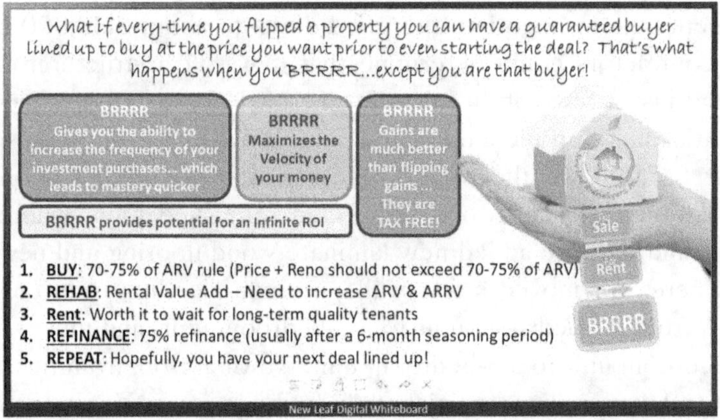

This blew Dan's mind. As Kimo continued with more project details, Dan listened to George's mentor in awe. He found it odd to think of his mentor having his own mentor. Dan was fascinated with this concept, and the more he thought about it, the more it excited him. It validated that he, too, without having all the answers yet, could eventually be a mentor to people just starting out, just like George was a mentor to him, and Kimo a mentor to George. Then, maybe a few new investors that Dan mentored would find it their purpose to continue to mentor the generations to follow. The impact, the complete change in direction for entire families for generations to come, was all starting in this room.

CHAPTER 21:

Your Financial Freedom, Then Your Legacy

Dear Reader,
Dan's story is not over. It is just beginning. We will continue that story in another book that details the magic of the Legacy Dinner Club. However, let's pause and bring you into this story for now. We added many different characters into this book and included each for a reason. If you search long enough, you are in this book. You are one of these characters at some point in their journey. Which character do you connect with most? The answer to that question may help you figure out your next step in real estate investing. As a free bonus for completing this book, you can create your own customized financial freedom plan here: **www.omnitheinvestorguy.com/resources/**

Scan the QR Code to go to the resources site

Caregiver and hospice nurse Bronnie Ware wrote a book with the insights accumulated and lessons learned from the many patients she cared for towards the end of their lives. Those findings were eventually published in the book *The Top 5 Regrets of the Dying*. Here is a list of those top 5 regrets.

1. I wish I had the courage to live a life true to myself, not the life others expected of me
2. I wish I hadn't worked so hard
3. I wish I had the courage to express my feelings
4. I wish I had stayed in touch with my friends
5. I wish I had let myself be happier

When we read that book, and as we look at this list now, we couldn't help but feel that each regret, different in its own right, does have a common thread tying them together, and that is the lack of choice or the lack of freedom--the lack of financial freedom to be more precise. If we restated these regrets through the lens of financial freedom, they would look something like this:

1. I wish I had the financial freedom that would have made it easier for me to live a life true to myself, not the life others expected of me.
2. I wish I had achieved financial freedom earlier in life so that I didn't need to work so hard later in life.
3. I wish I had the financial freedom that would have given me the confidence and security to always express my true feelings without the worry of possible employment or financial repercussions.
4. I wish I had the financial freedom that would have afforded me the time and the means to stay in touch with my friends.
5. I wish I had the financial freedom that would have afforded me the time and the means to focus more on what was truly important in life, which would have allowed me to let myself be happier.

In a book about financial freedom, money, and wealth, it may sound odd for us to tell you that money does not matter. But that is the case.

Money truly does not matter. It is freedom that is most important. Yet, oddly enough, those who do not care about, and consequently do not focus on money, wealth, and passive income, are the ones that often must worry about money the most their entire lives.

Those who focus intensely and intentionally on building passive income and wealth for a period will be the ones who will have the freedom not to worry or care about money. We are never truly free until we have financial freedom by achieving our passive income number. We are captive to our needs: our need for food, for shelter, for entertainment, for things, and ultimately, our need for employment to be able to pay for our needs.

Lastly, this story weaves in the most important lesson, which is essential for any new real estate investor to be successful. That is to belong to a community of like-minded investors committed to helping each other grow, impact, thrive, and who are willing to hold each other accountable to specific goals. These communities have great leaders, mentors, and members who provide education and value at minimal or no cost to members. These communities are built on a mindset of abundance, not scarcity. They understand the opportunities are endless, and the more like-minded, successful investors there are in the group, the greater the opportunities will be that will present themselves to its members. No one can do this alone. We all need a team. We all need a community to be successful.

Go find your tribe today.

Until our next journey together with Dan, Julie and Sarah, we wish you prosperity, health, and financial freedom.

If you would like to see if there is a Cash-Flow Breakfast Club or a Legacy Dinner Club in your area, or if you want to look into starting up a club in your area, go to **www.omnitheinvestorguy.com/Clubs**

ABOUT THE AUTHORS

Omni, Chara, and their three kids own and operate New Leaf Redevelopers, their family real estate investing company. Although they tackle many different investment projects, their primary focus has been to purchase vacant and barely habitable properties, fix them up to be the nicest property on the block, then rent them out at affordable rates.

As a family-run business, they also make it a point to keep their three kids (all under the age of thirteen) engaged in each real estate project to teach them the ins and outs of real estate transactions, investment deals, and firsthand experience with financial education.

Omni has been a real estate investor, broker, and coach for nearly 20 years. His real estate career started in Hawaii, where he grew up. Over the last 10+ years, he and his family have lived in Northern Virginia. They have been very active in growing their real estate investment portfolio and growing a top-performing real estate team and office in Loudoun County, Virginia. With a passion for building wealth and helping others achieve financial freedom, Omni has coached hundreds of real estate investors, real estate agents, and clients alike to create and execute a plan to grow their real estate business, investment portfolio, or both.

With a hyper-focus on building wealth and passive income through real estate investing, Omni is committed to helping as many people as possible stop **needing** to *earn* money, start down the path of *creating* money, and set up what he calls "PIFL" or Passive Income For Life.

Omni has been a keynote speaker and presenter on these topics hundreds of times. However, his focus and passion is one-on-one coaching. Contact Omni today if you are interested in having him as a guest presenter or speaker at your next event or if you are interested in a free coaching session to help you start, grow or scale your real estate agent or real estate investor business.

SOCIAL DISTANCE
INVESTING!
MULTI-FAMILY
CASHFLOW

New Leaf Investor
Power Team
?
CEO
IT &
Accounting
I WALK AROUND LIKE I'M OK
BUT DEEP DOWN INSIDE...
I WANT TO BUY 4 MORE
HOUSES
#AddictedToREI
#WeichertLouisiana
Weichert
Mandatory reading
CEO